# REHABILITATION AND COMMUNITY CARE

## STEPHEN PILLING

# LONDON AND NEW YORK

First published in 1991
by Routledge
11 New Fetter Lane, London EC4P 4EE

Simultaneously published in the USA and Canada
by Routledge
a division of Routledge, Chapman and Hall Inc.
29 West 35th Street, New York, NY 10001

© 1991 Stephen Pilling

Typeset by Witwell Ltd, Southport

Printed in Great Britain by Mackays of Chatham PLC, Kent

*British Library Cataloguing in Publication Data*
Pilling, Stephen
Rehabilitation and community care. - (Strategies for
mental health).
1. Great Britain. Mentally ill persons. Community
treatment
I. Title   II. Series
362.20425

*Library of Congress Cataloging in Publication Data*
Pilling, Stephen, 1955-
Rehabilitation and community care/Stephen Pilling.
p.    cm.    (Strategies for mental health)
Includes bibliographical references.
Includes index.
1. Community mental health services.   2. Mentally ill-
-Rehabilitation.   I. Title.   II. Series.
[DNLM: 1. Community Mental Health Services.   2. Mental
Disorders-rehabilitation.   WM 30 P641r]
RA790.P44   1991
362.2'2—dc20
DNLM/DLC
for Library of Congress                    90-8719
                                              CIP

ISBN 0-415-05817-1
0-415-01067-5 (pbk)

# CONTENTS

# ACKNOWLEDGEMENTS

I am grateful for the help and advice I have received from a number of colleagues over the years. The members of the Psychology Departments of Bexley and the Whittington Hospitals have done much to sustain and encourage my interest in rehabilitation. The staff and patients of Friern Hospital have played an important part in the writing of this book and the staff of that hospital's library deserve thanks for the tolerance they have shown for my tendency to hoard their books. I am grateful to John Cape and Paul Beard who respectively encouraged me first to come to Islington and then to stay, and for the opportunities that have stemmed from my time there. I have also benefited greatly from work with many colleagues in the mental health services in Islington over the past five years. In particular, the good sense and support of the members of the Transitional Team has done much to help me retain my sense of perspective. A particular mention should be made of Paul Clifford, Tony Lavender and Rob Leiper whose contribution is most obvious in Chapter 8 which relies heavily on our joint work on the QUARTZ system. Their contribution, however, goes well beyond that of a single chapter. My final acknowledgement is to Judy Leibowitz without whom it is certain this book would not have been written. She has encouraged me at all times and given much of her own time. So it is with much love and gratitude that I dedicate this book to her.

# EDITOR'S INTRODUCTION

The thesaurus gives 'cure', 'therapy', 'treatment' as alternatives to the word 'rehabilitation'. None of them quite fits, so we are left with a rather ugly word to describe a rather serious and complex issue: the system of care that we have, want to have, want to develop, for long-term mentally ill people. Questions arise immediately: Who are those people? What do they want? What do they need? What can the professionals do for them? What can others do for them? What has been done for them/with them in the past and what should be done and how in future? The issues are political, historical, sociological, psychological, and Stephen Pilling addresses them all in this book.

With health service and social services reforms having acquired a speed which leaves most planners and practitioners at least dizzy, the whole system of 'rehabilitation and community care' has been thrown into some chaos. The values and concepts of, for example, residential and day services, team work, community services have developed over many years. The danger is now that we lose them in the quick changes that are erupting all around us. It is therefore absolutely vital to publicise them in a practical way, so that practitioners can hold on to them in stormy seas.

This volume is a practical guide to the complex issues in work with long-term mentally ill people. It does justice to the complexities, always trying to be balanced rather than black and white, while giving practical strategies throughout. And this is how it must be. We are looking at an area where systems and human beings have an enormous degree of control over the lives of other human beings. History has shown us the possible disastrous results that 'power over' with the wrong values can have. Systems of care for disadvantaged and weak groups in our society need to protect the recipients of those services as well as the care givers. Those systems need to be value-based, balanced, realistic and scientific in order to provide a framework for the actions of individuals and groups.

Stephen Pilling's book gives the reader such a value-based framework plus the action plans needed for the service. A thorough definition of 'long-term mental illness' and the history of rehabilitation lead to the formulation of ten principles for such services in Chapter 1. And this list of principles is one of the many checklists throughout the book which form the basis for the reader's thinking, planning and action. Many of the following chapters have a wider appeal than just rehabilitation, especially the ones on 'teamwork', 'families' and 'quality assurance'. All in all this is a practical, value-based handbook with material that is relevant for all people who work in institutional caring services.

*Reinhard Kowalski*

# Chapter One

# INTRODUCING REHABILITATION

## INTRODUCTION

This book is about the rehabilitation of people with long-term mental illness. The nature and severity of the disabilities faced by these people are such that specialised services are required to meet their needs. It is the means by which these services are provided that is the primary concern of the book. The focus on such special needs should not, however, obscure the fact that the basic needs and aspirations of people with long-term mental illness are no different from those of any other citizen; that is to live with dignity, to have a say in shaping one's own life and to share the experience of life with others. The task of all those working in rehabilitation is to help people with long-term mental illness meet such needs and aspirations and to support them when they fall short of their goals.

## AN INDIVIDUAL'S EXPERIENCE

Brian is a 55-year-old man living with five others in a group home. He has lived there for four years following his discharge from a large psychiatric hospital after a ten-year stay. Brian requires considerable help with his self-care and if he is not reminded about having a wash or changing his clothes then he is unlikely to do either. His physical health is not good; he has recurrent chest problems and is under-weight. He suffers from schizophrenia which was first diagnosed thirty years ago. He is continually troubled by auditory hallucinations which distress him considerably. He receives a two-weekly injection of long-acting phenothiazines which provides partial relief from his more distressing psychiatric symptoms. He finds too much close contact with others in the house threatening and so spends a good deal of his time in his bedroom or out of the house, usually travelling on the buses. He has not worked for over thirty years and has great difficulty structuring his time. He occasionally attends a local day centre but finds it very difficult to concentrate on any activity. He has no social contacts outside the group home and day centre apart from a monthly visit to his sister.

Brian's difficulties are in many ways typical of those faced by long-term mentally ill people, whether they are long-term patients in large mental hospitals or have been resident in the community for many years. He needs help with his personal care and his physical health is poor. He is still troubled by psychiatric symptoms despite continued medication. He is socially isolated and unable to occupy himself constructively during the day. The development of his problems is the result of a complex interaction between a biological vunerability, his personal and social skills and society's response (including his care and treatment) to his problems. Understanding his disability requires the consideration of a number of factors and it is to this matter that we next turn.

## WHAT IS LONG-TERM MENTAL ILLNESS?

If the above question had been asked of someone forty years ago it would have been possible to describe long-term mental illness as a condition affecting the residents of the large mental hospitals. Although this would not have been an accurate answer then, it is totally inaccurate today when a small percentage of long-term mentally ill people have never been admitted to hospital and a much larger group make only limited use of hospital services (Sturt *et al.*, 1982). Nor is it possible to restrict the term to people suffering from a particular psychiatric disorder. Although chronic schizophrenia is the most common (about 70 per cent of beds for functionally ill people in the large mental hospitals are occupied by people with schizophrenia) and the most debilitating of chronic mental illnesses, to limit the definition of long-term mental illness to chronic schizophrenia would be to ignore the disabilities faced by many people. One solution is include a wider range of diagnostic groups and whilst this resolves some of the difficulty it is not entirely successful. A wider view of the problem is required. Bacharach (1988), in a useful review, lists three factors to be considered when defining long-term mental illness:

*Chronicity* - that is the length of time since the onset of the disorder (such a defintion allows for fluctuations in the symptoms of the illness, which may at times remit).

*Diagnosis* - this may or may not be limited only to psychotic disorders and should also take into account the fact that illness may persist in the absence of the original florid symptoms.

*Disability* - the extent to which a person is impaired in the primary activities of daily living.

The definition of long-term mental illness is, therefore, the product of a complex interaction between these three factors of which disability usually plays the primary role. The difficulty in fully understanding the nature of the interaction between these factors reflects a lack of knowledge about the development and course of severe mental illness. At the present time the stress-diathesis model (Liberman, 1988) is perhaps the most useful model we have for thinking about the course of long-term mental illness and explaining the wide variation in outcomes over the years. It proposes an underlying biological vulnerability which results, in the presence of stressors, in an exacerbation of symptoms and disabilities. Stressors can include changes in both internal (or physical) state, for example, as a result of illness or drug abuse, and external circumstances, for example, the loss of a job or a change of accommodation. Both underlying vulnerability and stressors can be moderated in their effects by a number of protective factors. These factors include drug treatments, the personal skills and resources of an individual and the degree to which the environment supports an individual.

The determination of the appropriate degree of disability, chronicity or diagnostic group which leads to a definition of long-term mental illness, will reflect not only professional assessment and the client's views, but also the level of disability and distress which society finds acceptable. The availability of resources, the cost of those resources and the problems presented to the wider community by the long-term mentally ill person, will all play a part in determining what is acceptable. The accurate assessment of individual need and society's view of an acceptable response is central to determining the criteria which govern access to services. A major concern of the Griffiths report on community care (Griffiths, 1988) was with assessment and access to services. The implementation of the White Paper *Caring for People* (DHSS, 1989) that followed the Griffiths Report, may result in the establishment of more criteria-based systems for access to services than presently exist. Bacharach (1988) describes in some detail, the consequences of the adoption of various criteria for access to services by long-term mentally ill people in the United States. In the United States, where criteria based definitions of disorders are often central to obtaining services, definitions such as the one given below are common.

> The chronically mentally ill are defined as those persons whose emotional or behavioural functioning is so impaired as to interfere grossly with their capacity to remain in the community without supportive treatment or services of a long-term or indefinite duration. The mental disability is severe and persistent, resulting in a long-term limitation of their functional capacity for primary activities of daily living such as interpersonal relationships, homemaking and self-care, employment, or recreation. The mental disability may limit their ability to seek or receive local, state, or federal assistance such as housing, medical and dental care, rehabilitation services, income assistance and food stamps, or protective services. Although persons with primary diagnoses of mental retardation or organic brain syndrome frequently have similar problems or limitations, they are not to be included in this definition.
>
> (quoted in Bacharach, 1988)

In Britain there has been less concern with precise definitions of chronic mental illness than with describing the difficulties people experience and relating these to service usage. One important distinction is that made between the primary, secondary and tertiary effects of mental illness (Wing and Morris, 1981). The primary effects are seen as those which are inherent to the illness, e.g. hallucinations; the secondary effects are those which arise as a result of an inability to perform some activity because of the illness, e.g. lack of attention to personal hygiene; the tertiary effects are those which arise from the negative response of others to a long-term mentally ill person, e.g. stigmatisation or the consequences of long-term social disadvantage. Another distinction is that made between positive and negative symptoms. Postive symptoms can be taken to refer to clear abnormalities such as delusions and hallucinations, whereas negative symptoms refer to behavioural deficits such as self-neglect and social withdrawal. Most rehabilitation interventions are concerned with negative symptoms.

In the context of service usage it is also helpful to be familiar with the following terminology (Wing and Morris, 1981):

*The Old Long-Stay* – that is those people who have been in psychiatric hospital typically for five or more years. (See the Christie-Brown *et al.* (1977) study described below for a more detailed description of this group.)

*The New Long-Stay* – that is those people who have been in psychiatric hospital for more than one year but less than five. (A more detailed description is given in the Mann and Cree (1976) study referred to below.)

*The New Long-Term* – that is those people who, whilst not long-term in-patients, have a high and continuing need for a range of services including hospital admission. (Such a group are described below with reference to the work of Sturt *et al.* (1982) and Wykes *et al.* (1982).)

Stigma was identified as a tertiary consequence of mental illness and it is unfortunately true that the very use of the words 'mental illness' can be stigmatising. As a result there has been considerable criticism of the term 'long-term mental illness' because amongst other things it emphasises continued dependence and the medical model. The question, therefore, arises as to whether it should be dropped. The position taken in this book is that the term, carelessly and thoughtlessly applied, can be damaging, but in the absence of suitable alternatives it remains the most useful option available. Importantly it serves as a reminder that whatever the course of the disability, the difficulties originate with a mental illness which will almost invariably have had a

5

profound impact on the sufferer and their family. Generally the phrase will be used throughout the book, but on occasions terms such as mental disability or chronic mental illness will be used and can be assumed to be synonymous.

## THE EXTENT OF LONG-TERM MENTAL ILLNESS

Whilst the terms and categories described above have value as a kind of 'shorthand' for describing broad requirements for services, it should be remembered that they are of little value in understanding individual needs, particularly where individuals with severe disabilities have not been regular users of services. This will increasingly be the case as services move towards a more dispersed community model. The methods by which more detailed assessments of individual need can be made will be the subject of subsequent chapters. For the moment we can gain some overall estimate of the extent of need by reviewing those studies which have looked at various populations of people with long-term mental illness.

Christie-Brown *et al.* (1977) surveyed 220 'old long-stay' patients in a large mental hospital. They had an average age of 54 years, with virtually half the population falling in the 51–65 years age group. Seventy-two per cent were male, only 8 per cent were married and they had been in hospital for average of 21 years. The majority (67 per cent) had a diagnosis of schizophrenia and 20 per cent had significant physical disabilities. Their lives were, in the main, centred around the hospital with only 20 per cent having visited someone outside the hospital in the six months prior to the survey. Although only one-third were felt to require hospital care, the vast majority needed some form of supervised care, their age and physical frailty indicating that such needs were likely to increase. Ford *et al.* (1987) reported on the population of another large mental hospital and described an older and frailer group of residents with twice the percentage of patients in the over-75 age group than reported by Christie-Brown *et al.* (1977). This may reflect a general trend towards discharge of some of the more able of the old-long stay population, as well the increasing age and frailty of those that remain. It suggests that the needs of the remaining long-stay population have increased and there is a need for a higher level of care,

6

including physical care, if these people are to be cared for in the community in the manner in which Christie-Brown *et al.* indicated.

Mann and Cree (1976) looked specifically at the 'new long-stay' population. They surveyed 400 patients, from 15 different hospitals, who had been in-patients for a period of between one and three years. The majority were female (52 per cent) and the most common diagnosis was schizophrenia (44.4 per cent). Significant physical disability was present in almost 16 per cent of the group surveyed. Approximately one-third of the group were assessed as requiring some form of longer term hospital care and it was estimated that perhaps half of this group would move on to some form of less intensive care with further rehabilitation. They suggested, based on cautious estimates, that 17 places per 100,000 of the local population would be needed for this group.

Sturt *et al.* (1982) and Wykes *et al.* (1982) looked at 158 individuals using a range of residential and day services, in a well resourced London borough (Camberwell) with a population of approximately 150,000. They included individuals who had been in contact with the services for over one year, but excluded those who had been in-patients for over a year. The average age of the group was 52 years, 60 per cent of them were female and 47 per cent had a diagnosis of schizophrenia. Almost half (47 per cent) had 'quite serious physical disabilities', a finding which was fairly consistent across all age groupings. Three-quarters of the group had been in contact with the psychiatric services for over 10 years and only 2.5 per cent had never been admitted to a psychiatric hospital. Only 26 per cent were judged to be living independently, the rest were receiving some form of support in their residence. The results of these two studies have largely been confirmed by a more recent survey by Brewin *et al.* (1988). Brewin *et al.* also reported that 44 per cent of the population surveyed were identified as having one or more unmet need. Sturt *et al.* (1982) calculated the prevalence of this group to be 139 per 100,000 giving an estimate of around 240 in an 'average' health district of around 200,000 people. By way of comparison a further 118 per 100,000 were in contact with day and residential services for less than one year and 160 per 100,000 were long-stay in-patients.

It can be appreciated from the above figures that the majority of long-term mentally ill people live outside hospital and indeed did so before the renewed drive towards community based care. It is interesting to note that even in a borough as well served as Camberwell 44 per cent of new long-term mentally ill people had at least one unmet need. In other less well resourced services it seems reasonable to assume that a significant number of individuals living in the community lead lives as impoverished as many patients on negelected long-stay wards.

## THE DEVELOPMENT OF MENTAL HEALTH CARE

Although the current focus of mental health care is moving away from mental hospitals, they have played the central role in the provision of care during the past hundred years and, given the present rate of closure of the large hospitals, will continue to do so into the next century. The large mental hospitals were the creation of Victorian public spirit and humanitarian concern. In the mid-nineteenth century public concern about the treatment of mentally ill people, particularly in the tuberculosis-ridden private madhouses of London's East End, led to the establishment of the county asylums, which still provide most of the long-term psychiatric care today. Pioneers, such as John Conolly (1847), set out to establish a new way of treating mentally ill people which recognised their rights to treatment with dignity and was optimistic about their potential for recovery. Much was achieved by Conolly, Maudsley and others in the later part of the nineteenth century. Unfortunately, these institutions became victims of their success, quickly becoming overcrowded and, by the time of the First World War, when the mental hospital population was proportionally at its peak, they performed a purely custodial function. The optimism of Conolly and his contemporaries had evaporated. It was not until the end of the Second World War that any major developments occurred. The war had seen a number of successful experiments in social psychiatry (Clark, 1977) and this along with a renewed social concern and economic prosperity brought about what is often characterised as a revolution in psychiatry. The 1950s also saw the introduction of the phenothiazines, psychotropic drugs which were to have a significant impact on the treatment of the major mental illnesses. Much of the pioneering work in psychiatric rehabilitation by such people as Douglas Bennett and Donal Early began during this time and the psychosocial model of psychiatric rehabilitation they developed continues to be the pre-eminent model today (Bennett, 1983).

The work of these social psychiatrists met with a good deal of success. Active rehabilitation programmes, including the development of Industrial Therapy, saw many people discharged from the hospitals. For example, the hospital population dropped from approximately 154,000 in 1954 to 76,000 in 1979 (Shepherd, 1984). In addition to the reduction in hospital beds there began the development of a range of community services including day hospitals and group homes, which provided community based treatment and support for mentally ill people. However, the 1970s saw a slow down in the process of dein-stitutionalisation. A number of factors explain this slow down. First, overly optimistic estimates were made of the level of community support needed by some individuals, with the result that inadequate and uncoordinated community support was provided. Secondly, the needs of those people who remained in hospital were very different from those discharged in the 1950s and 1960s. They required not only more support, but also different models of community support services than had proved effective for the first groups of patients discharged. Thirdly, the 1970s saw a contraction in resources available to the public and voluntary sectors and this undoubdtedly had an effect on service's capacity to care.

## THE NEW MOVE TO COMMUNITY CARE

The 1980s saw a renewed drive to close the large mental hopitals. This resulted from, first, a wider move within society against institutional care; not just for long-term mentally ill people but for a range of disabled groups including the mentally handi-capped, the chronically sick elderly and the physically disabled. (A major force behind this development was the recognition and promotion of the rights of these disabled groups.) Secondly, there had been increasing difficulties in running the large mental hospitals effectively. These difficulties included the problems of chronic understaffing (arising from problems both of recriut-ment and retention), rising unit costs (as more patients move out of the large institutions then the *per capita* costs of those remaining increase) and the fact that most of the resources tied up in the institutions could not be released for community services, further delaying their development. Indeed a disproportionate amount of these resources was required to simply service increasingly delapidated building stock. It is also clear that concern about the overall cost of community-based services has been central to the debate. This has led to what may be characterised as an 'unholy alliance' between those concerned with the possible, if illusory, cost saving potential of community care, with its associated shift of the burden of care away from direct state provision to a more dispersed group of individuals or services, and those who see it as an opportunity to develop a comprehensive community-based service.

Community care in the 1980s became a matter of public interest, with genuine concern being expressed about the level of service provision for a range of disabled people. Unfortunately, this public concern has often taken the form of a rather sterile debate about whether hospital care or community-based care is better, ignoring both existing research on the efficacy of community-based care and the continuing interdependence of hospital and community services. The level of public and political interest has led to a number of goverment sponsored investigations; two of the most important being the Audit Commission Report (1986) and the Griffiths Report *Community Care: an Agenda for Action* (Griffiths, 1988). The Audit Commission identified a lack of coordination of services with consequent failures in both the planning and implementation of services for people with a range of chronic disabilities. The Griffiths Report proposes a radical reorganisation of services for a wide range of disabled people to be implemented over the next few years. The report distinguishes between social and medical care. The responsibility for medical care remaining with the health authorities but with primary responsibility for social care being given to local authorities. Much work still needs to be done to clarify the distinction between social and medical care as the reality of the distinction may well not be as clear in practice as the Griffiths Report or the subsequent White Paper (DHSS, 1989) assume. There is also to be a clear responsibility on local authorities to assess needs for care and then purchase it, rather than provide it.

The implementation of the Griffiths recommendations means a gradual shift in resources away from mental health services in the NHS, assuming, of course, that the present policy of closure of the large mental hospitals continues.

## THE CASE AGAINST HOSPITAL CLOSURE

The debate on community care has often been little more than an argument for or against hospital closure (for example, Kendell, 1989). Concern has been expressed that no community-based service will ever be able to care for the most disabled of the long-term mentally ill and this has been advanced as a reason for not closing the large mental hospitals. Whilst it is true that a number of long-term mentally ill people will continue to require hospital care there is no evidence that this needs to be provided on the large mental hospital site. Indeed, there is evidence to suggest that services for such people can be developed away from large mental hospitals (Wykes, 1982). Garety *et al.*, (1988) describe a ten-year follow-up study of a hospital–hostel which demonstrates how many of the most disturbed and disabled of a large mental hospital population can be cared for outside of the long-stay mental hospital.

The need for asylum is also cited as an important function of the large mental hospitals which will not be provided by the new community-based services. The discussion is often clouded by a lack of understanding of what is meant by the term asylum, primarily arising from what Bacharach (1983) has called a confusion of 'program substance with geography'. There is little evidence to support the assertion that asylum, when needed, must be provided on a large mental hopspital site. (The issue of need for asylum will be taken up more fully in Chapter 5.) A further argument advanced against the hospital closure programmes is that there are insufficient resources to develop comprehensive community-based services and therefore closures should be delayed until these resources are available. Whilst it is undoubtedly the case that resources are limited, it is also true that, given that resources are not infinite, it is increasingly difficult to justify tying up a disproportionate amount of the resources for mental health care in the large mental hospitals. The large mental hospitals use a higher proportion of their

11

budget on support services (i.e. building maintenance, heating, portering, etc.) and a lower proportion on direct client care than community-based services. Even if the financial resources were available to develop community-based services independently of the financial resources currently tied up in the large mental hospitals, it is very unlikely that other resources, such as appropriately experienced staff, would be available.

Closely linked to the concern about lack of resources is the fear that there will be a shift in the burden of care from the statutory services to informal carers such as relatives (Lefley, 1989). In the United Kingdom, the National Schizophrenia Fellowship (NSF) (an organisation representing the families of people suffering from schizophrenia) and in the United States, similar organisations such as the National Alliance for the Mentally Ill, have campaigned vigorously against the closure of the mental hospitals, fearing that the burden of care will fall on their shoulders. This is a very real and serious concern but unfortunately, as with much of the community care debate, it has quickly led to polarisation so that the evidence which shows that good community-based services produce no increase in family burden (for example, Hoult and Reynoulds, 1984) are largely ignored. A major responsibility for the lack of support from organisations like the NSF for community care lies with those proponents of community care who have chosen to ignore the legitimate interests of families. For, despite the pejorative and pathogenic labels all too easily applied to families by a range of mental health professionals, they are primarily responsible for the community care of the vast majority of long-term mentally ill people and as such are a major and neglected group. (Methods of working with families and carers will be discussed in Chapter 7.)

There has also been considerable concern that the closure of the mental hospitals will lead to a large increase in the number of homeless mentally ill people; a situation which has arisen in parts of the United States but about which there is little firm evidence in the United Kingdom (Priest *et al.*, 1985). It is important to distinguish between those homeless persons with mental illness who are unsupported as a result of existing service inadequacy and those who are homeless as a result of hospital closure programmes. In the current political climate such clarity is often lacking (for example, Timms and Fry, 1989). Current evaluations of hospital closure programmes show very few patients disappear onto the streets or elsewhere. For example, Thornicroft (1989) reports only 3 out of 161 patients discharged under a hospital closure scheme were untraceable after one year. Whatever their origins, homeless mentally ill people are a poorly served group and represent a significant challenge to any community-based service. Methods of addressing their needs will be returned to in Chapter 5.

Finally, the opposition of certain professional groups to the closure of mental hospitals cannot be underestimated. At its best this opposition stems from a real concern that community-based services will not adequately care for particular sections of the large mental hospital population. At its worst it places professional self-interest ahead of the development of services. It is often difficult to disentangle these two concerns, not only for the dispassionate observer but also for the professionals. The clear association of professional development with service development needs to be pointed out. Much of this opposition could be channelled into more positive support if staff at all levels were involved in the process of the hospital closure, a point which will be taken up in Chapter 2.

Rehabilitation is, however, not defined by the setting in which it occurs. Whatever the outcome of the debate on hospital closure, rehabilitation will continue in both hospital and community settings and it is to the ideas underpinning good rehabilitation practice that we now turn.

## DEFINING REHABILITATION

Our understanding of the process of rehabilitation varies not only with the tasks presented to a service but also in response to prevailing economic and social conditions of the society in which the service operates. Such changing conditions are reflected in the differing ideologies of care that are determined by a society's underlying beliefs and values. It is important to acknowledge such values because otherwise it is difficult to develop clear principles for a rehabilitation service. A consideration of the three definitions of rehabilitation set out below may help to clarify matters:

utilization of means which are as culturally normative as possible in order to establish and/or maintain behaviour and characteristics which are as culturally normative as possible.

(Wolfensberger, 1980)

the process of helping a physically or psychiatrically disabled person to make the best use of his residual abilities in order to function in as normal an environment as possible.

(Bennett, 1978)

philosophically . . . rehabilitation is directed at increasing the strengths of clients so that they can achieve their maximum potential for independent living and meaningful careers.

(Anthony *et al.*, 1981)

Normalisation theory (more recently referred to as Social Role Valourization by Wolfensberger (1983)) was developed by Wolfensberger and his colleagues (see Flynn and Nitsch (1980) for a comprehensive overview). It emerged in North America in the 1970s as a major ideological force. Its central concern was with the rights of mentally disabled people to live a full life in the community, particularly those who had been discharged from the large institutions. As the term Social Role Valourization implies, the social value that is given by society to the experience of long-term mental illness or being resident in a large mental hospital is seen as key to understanding much of the difficulty faced by disabled individuals. The ultimate goal of a mental health service (or any other human service) is the enhancement of the value of the social role assigned to those individuals who use the service and who, in part as a consequence of doing so, are at risk of social devaluation. There are two major sub-goals for services, one concerned with the enhancement of an individual's social image, the other concerned with the enhancement of an individual's personal competency. At the practical level this results, in the case of social image, in an emphasis on the physical setting (e.g. is it an attractive building), on the language and symbols used to describe the service or its users (e.g. 'lunatics' or 'consumers') or on the presence or absence of age-appropriate activities (e.g. cuddly teddy bears for mentally handicapped adults). In the case of competency enhancement, it is concerned with ensuring services provide opportunities for valued social experiences (for example, a trip to the theatre with a friend, if necessary learning apppropriate skills in order to achieve this task). In addition, the normalisation movement has been closely associated with a concern for individual rights; one of the most obvious effects of which has been the growth of an advocacy movement where the representation of individuals' needs for services have been taken up in a number of ways (see Chapter 8 for further discussion of the varying models of advocacy).

Normalisation theory can be criticised for its over-emphasis on the social creation of disability as the central factor in explaining the development and maintenance of the problems faced by mentally ill people and the poor quality services they tradition-ally receive. It can also be criticised for its lack of specificity regarding individual care and treatment. Nevertheless, it has served to highlight very important issues regarding the social value given to the role of mentally disabled people in society and draws attention to the images, all too often negative, presented by the services they receive.

In contrast Bennett's (1978) definition places more emphasis on individual skills (see Watts and Bennett (1983a) for a com-prehensive overview). It stresses the work to be done with individuals, in particular the development of individual skills and the importance of aiding individuals in adapting to the demands of their environment or, where necessary, the creation of specially designed environments. This reflects the develop-ment of Bennett's work in the 1950s and 1960s when the central concern was with the resettlement of large numbers of relatively able long-stay patients into the community. In contrast to normalisation, which places a very high premium on integ-ration, it promotes the design and establishment of segregated environments where this can be justified by the opportunities provided for the development of individual skills, appropriate social roles or the provision of long-term support. It affords a less central position to the social consequences of the negative image associated with the use of segregated services. The approach is influenced by theoretical views of adult socialisation (Brim and Wheeler, 1966). The concern with social adaptation is important in understanding the constantly changing nature of the problems faced in rehabilitation. As the environment changes, which includes not only the physical environment but people as well, so a person needs to adapt. A failure to do so (and it must be remembered that long-term mentally ill people may for a number of reasons find adaptation difficult) results in stress. This stress, as was seen in the earlier discussion of the stress-diathesis model, can lead to increased disability. With the emphasis on social roles many activities of life legitimately become the concern of rehabilitation. The need to consider a diverse range of social roles is useful as it helps to counteract the general tendency in psychiatry to emphasise weakness at the expense of strength; a tendency exaggerated by the fact that many rehabilitation professionals are schooled in the diagnosis and treatment of pathologies.

The definition of Anthony *et al.* (1981) has a good deal in common with that of Bennett. They both place particular emphasis on the development of individual strengths. Although the focus is again on the individual; the orientation of Anthony *et al.* is somewhat different from that of Bennett, reflecting the different contexts in which the ideas developed. Anthony *et al.*'s work developed in the United States where much rehabilitation, and vocational rehabilitation in particular, has developed outside of a health service context. Although acknowledging the importance of the psychiatric symptomatology and treatment, they place a greater emphasis on an educative, skills-based model which is less concerned with the provision of specialist environments and more with how the individual may, with the help of others, begin to modify his own environment. Such concerns reflect their work with a less disabled group than many long-stay patients.

However, despite their differences in emphasis all the models share two key components:

1 The promotion of interventions which are aimed at helping individuals develop or re-learn skills and role competencies.
2 Modifications to the social and physical environment in order to preserve or enhance functioning in spite of continuing disabilities.

Rehabilitation, therefore, encompasses a wide range of activities, from the treatment of symptoms to the development of highly specialised living environments. At its centre is a recognition of the enduring nature of some disabilities (Shepherd, 1988a). Such recognition should not, however, be taken as a pessimistic acceptance of the status quo which does not acknowledge the possibility of any personal development. Rehabilitation activities such as attendance at a sheltered workshop or the development of self-care skills can provide real opportunities for personal growth and development (Strauss, 1986). However, recognising the possibility of personal development should not be translated into a demand for a constant increase in an individual's independence. Progress will not always be straightforward or possible and there will be setbacks despite the best endeavours. Learning about rehabilitation is about acquiring the necessary skills and knowledge to cope with such events.

## PRINCIPLES FOR A REHABILITATION SERVICE

What follows is a set of principles which reflect the contribution of the various ideas discussed above. Their purpose is to provide a framework with which to evaluate the rehabilitation practice that is described in this book and to act as a guide to good practice. It is important to remember that principles should be seen as guides pointing in desirable directions. They should not be slavishly followed, as it is possible in certain settings that various principles may come into conflict, their purpose then being to try and help make such conflicts explicit and open to discussion and possible resolution. Failure to live up to them should not only be seen as a consequence of either limited resources or imagination but also as a reflection of the struggles inherent in rehabilitation.

1 The service should be based on a broad and comprehensive conception of human need which recognises clients' rights to full citizenship.
2 The service should value and promote the involvement of the client in all decisions and aim to provide real choice.
3 The service should promote the integration of its clients into their natural community.
4 The service should promote the development of normal patterns of life through the establishment of appropriate social roles.
5 The service should seek to maximise the independence of its users and build on their assets and support systems.

6 The service should be based on the assessment of individual need.

7 The service should be continuously evaluated in terms of its accessibility, acceptability, equity, comprehensibility, and cost-effectivness.

8 The service should aim to be comprehensive in the range of services it offers.

9 The service should be coordinated both within and across agencies.

10 The service should provide for and support the continued personal development of the client.

The rest of the book is now taken up with a discussion of some of the ways in which these principles can be put into practice.

# Chapter Two

# THE TRANSITION FROM HOSPITAL TO COMMUNITY

## INTRODUCTION

Hospital closures, in whole or part, will be a major means by which mental health services are established in the community and it is therefore necessary to devote a chapter to the topic. The closure of some hospital-based services is a necessary but not sufficient step towards the development of community care and there is real danger in seeing the development of community care as synonymous with that of hospital closure. It is important to recognise that all the problems of hospital or community care will not be solved by hospital closures. Community care involves more than the simple transfer of resources for one site to another, and hospital care, in some form, will continue to form a key component of any community-based service. (The role of hospital services in rehabilitation will be taken up more fully in Chapter 5).

This chapter has a particular concern with the active role direct care workers (that is all staff, at whatever level, who are concerned with the planning, implementation or monitoring of care or treatment) can take in the transition from hospital to community. All too often direct care workers withdraw from active involvement in the transitional process, feeling themselves to be on the receiving end of decisions about which they had not been consulted (alas this is often true). However, direct care workers, like service users, managers and funding agencies, are in Kingsley and Towell's (1988) term 'stakeholders'. This means they have a legitimate interest in the process and, as the term implies, suggests that their stake will not be simply given out but that it must be claimed. In the transition from hospital to community four main areas of activity for direct care workers emerge. They are listed below.

1 The assessment of patients for the move.
2 The preparation of patients for the move.
3 The preparation of staff for the move.
4 The preparation of the community for the move.

To be effective the work in these four areas must be fully integrated into the overall planning of the hospital closure, ensuring that the planning process stays 'alive', nurtured by feedback from all levels of the system. Of course, this is fine if you have a responsive planning system (or, indeed if you have anything that could be called a plan!) but if one does not exist it may be the responsibility of the direct care worker to argue for one. Towell and McAusland (1984) in their paper 'Psychiatric services in transiton' identify twenty key points to be addressed in the closure of a large mental hospital. They form a useful checklist to be used by any individual or organisation involved in the process of transition. Although developed primarily for planners and managers, the checklist (see Table 2.1) is useful to direct care workers in three ways. First, by providing clues to the kind of questions to be asked of senior staff. Secondly, by highlighting those parts of the transitional process in which direct care workers have a major contribution to make. Thirdly, by stimulating a discussion of what skills and training are required if these contributions are to be made.

The checklist provides a comprehensive overview of the transitional process and should raise a good number of questions in any service. There can, of course, be no attempt to answer these questions here; the intention rather is to stimulate debate about and concern with the whole transitional process. To direct care workers many of the above questions may seem irrelevant, but although they may not be involved in district or regional planning groups it is essential that they know of their existence and of the decisions thay are making. The rest of the chapter is now given over to those areas which impinge most directly on the direct care worker. In working through these areas it may help, on occasion, to think back to some of the questions that were raised by the checklist.

*Table 2.1*  Checklist for services in transition

---

*Questions to be asked at the Regional Level*
1  Is there any established guiding vision for future services based on an explicit statement of philosophy and principles?
2  Is there political backing for this vision at the authority level and a commitment to making resources available?
3  For the large mental hospitals, have inter-district mechanisms to coordinate the the reallocation of resources been established? Is responsibility for managing the redeployment of staff clear?
4  Is there an identifiable staff group providing the leadership required? Is there investment in the necessary skills for planning and implementing change?
5  Is there a real dialogue between planners and providers about opportunities and problems in achieving progress?

*Questions to be asked at the District/Local Authority Level.*
6  Is there a district planning forum with adequate representation from the local authority and voluntary sector?
7  Does this forum have agreed priorities which allow for innovation at a sufficiently 'near the ground' level to able to meet individual needs?
8  Is planning for real, that is, based on realistic financial and manpower assumptions with access to systematic data about future needs and demands for services?
9  Are the views of clients and the local community actively sought and incorporated into the current and future shape of the services?
10  Is planning free from the constraints of old and existing models and open to innovations?
11  Are planners and managers trying to work through rather than avoid the conflicts that arise throughout the transitional process?
12  Is the process informed by explicit evaluations of services for similar client groups?
13  Are relevant development and training opportunities provided for staff so that their full potential for contribution can be realised?
14  Are service objectives, client needs and resources carefully related? Is attention paid to maintaining the service once the novelty wears off?

*Questions to be asked at the level of Management of the Contracting Institution.*
15  Are relevant parts of the large mental hospital linked to the receiving district services?
16  Is there adequate communication and participation so that staff understand the plan to change and contribute to shaping the future?
17  Are appropriate personnel policies established to ensure a smooth transition?
18  Are there adequate resources to anticipate any increased demand from the institution throughout the closure process?
19  Do admission and retrenchment policies give institutional staff the chance to improve the services they provide?
20  Is the interest of those patients who have been in hospital for many years properly considered?

---

# ASSESSMENT FOR THE TRANSITION

There are two main purposes of assessment for the transition: assessment for planning and assessment of individual needs.

Whilst the purposes are distinct, it is possible, but neither necessary nor desirable in all cases, to employ the same method to achieve both purposes. Whatever method is chosen it is important that these two distinct aims are acknowledged. Before going on to describe the methods available, some important concepts underlying assessment will be considered. Although, the specific concern here is with the transitional process, the points made are applicable to most areas of assessment.

Whatever the purpose of assessment in rehabilitation it is essentially an attempt to measure or represent, in some form, individual need. Brewin *et al.* (1987) discuss the concept of need specifically in relation to the assessment of mentally ill people. They point out the considerable ambiguity that currently exists in the use of the term. A number of alternative conceptualisations, drawn from the work of Bradshaw (1972), are described, including patient-assessed and provider-assessed need; felt need (that which is only experienced) and expressed need (that which is experienced and communicated); normative need (that which is defined by expert judgement) and comparative need (which is defined by comparison to others). The reason for listing these varying conceptualisations is simply to emphasise that need is never solely based on facts alone but is always influenced by the underlying values and the judgements of those making the assessment.

However need is conceptualised, a key element in any assessment procedure concerns the nature of the interaction of the person being assessed with their environment or, put more simply, people behave differently in different situations. This complex interaction makes hospital-based assessment for community services difficult and a poor predictor of future success in community placement. As much work in rehabilitation is concerned with the provision of special environments (and this means not only the physical environment but also the resources available, both social and personal, within the wider environment) attempting to understand the nature of this interaction is vital. To take a rather crude example, an individual may have a severe skills deficit with respect to cooking. However, other factors, including the individual's own wishes and the availability of a suitably staffed group home, may result in the provision of an environment which doesn't require them to do

22

any cooking. The issue of environment and individual interaction, however, often occurs in more subtle ways. Hospitals are, at times to the detriment of individuals, remarkably tolerant of a range of behaviours to the extent that odd or anti-social behaviours which would result in severe problems in the community are ignored entirely. It can therefore be difficult to pick these up in any form of assessment in the hospital environment. (Hall (1984) reports a study where staff, working two per shift in a psychiatric ward, were able to observe only 15 per cent of a patient's daily life.) Equally, there are some functions of the hospital, often unacknowledged, which perform a vital supportive role. For example, the large reassuring presence of the hospital, with its implicit understanding of mental illness, may represent a valuable resource that an indivdual may struggle to find in a community setting. Therefore, whatever assessment methodology is used, there must be constant effort to understand in what way a particular environment both helps to shape and define need.

We are helped in our understanding of the role of the environment by those who have looked at the function of the mental hospital. Bacharach (1983), has set out what she considers to be the key functions of the mental hospital. They can be summarised as follows:

1 The provision of long-term treatment and care – including mental and physical care and its monitoring.
2 The provision of a place of safety – for either the patient who is stressed or the family who are overstretched.
3 The provision of long-term accommodation – at the most basic, a bed to sleep in.
4 The provision of social control – the removal of individuals who represent some threat to society and otherwise would be in prison or similar.
5 The provision of social and vocational help – through the presence of a number of services, e.g. occupational or industrial therapy.
6 The illusion of comprehensive care – so diverting the need for planning and expenditure.
7 The employment of mental health professionals – their training and professional development.

For those familiar with the large mental hospitals, it is not difficult to see where existing services fail to fulfil these functions. Yet, in her review of the progress made by the deinstitutionalisation programmes in the United States, Bacharach concludes that some of the most basic functions of treatment and asylum have often not been reprovided; there has, she writes, been a confusion of 'geography with program substance'. A consideration of the first five of the above functions helps to generate useful questions about the way in which the hospital environment helps or supports an individual and should be borne in mind when making any assessment. They are also useful as a framework for considering the overall adequacy of services that have been reprovided in community settings and offer a structure for integrating the disparate information that is collected as part of any assessment process.

Although Bacharach's framework is of value when considering the position of individuals, it is perhaps most effective for considering the overall reprovision of services. Clifford and Wolfson (1989) in the development of a system for the assessment of care environments, describe five dimensions of the environment. They are homeliness, social and personal care, containment, independence and social relationships. The last four of these dimensions have much in common with the first five functions of the mental hospital described by Bacharach (1983). They are briefly described below, as they refer to important aspects of the environment in a way which relates rather more directly to individual care.

*Personal and social care* – the degree to which the setting supervises an individual's care from personal hygiene through to the more social aspects of people's lives such as use of transport or submitting benefit claims.

*Containment* – the extent to which the setting tolerates and attempts to understand behavioural and psychological disturbance.

*Independence* – the extent to which the setting acknowledges and promotes the development of individual social functioning.

*Social relationships* – the extent to which the setting recognises the need for people to have regular contact with others and provides the opportunity to provide some sense of belonging to a community.

In the reprovision of any mental hospital service, care should be taken to avoid repeating the mistakes made in the United States, which Bacharach (1983) describes. For example, let us consider one function, that of social control, which can often be forgotten in the rush to develop community-based services. It is an important function, with some element of it usually enshrined in legislation. However, such a function can rest very uneasily with the more positively viewed (by health professionals at least) activities of treatment and rehabilitation. It would, however, be an error to imagine that this controlling role will simply disappear when the large hospitals close. Rather, it is important to acknowledge explicitly this function of the mental health services. A failure to do so could lead to both an increase in the number of seriously mentally ill people held inappropriately in prison and those who wander aimlessly on the streets of our major cities.

## Assessment methods

The above discussion provides a framework for the integration of information obtained from the assessment process. In considering the methods that may be adopted to collect such information a number of general points should be borne in mind. The first concerns what might be called the scientific properties of any assessment method. Essentially these are concerned with the reliability and validity of the measures. The reliability of a measure indicates the extent to which the method will produce a consistent result if used by different people to measure the same thing, and validity refers to the extent to which a measure accurately measures what it is intended to. There are times when reliability and validity are very important. For example, if you were measuring the change in a particular behaviour of the same group of patients, on a ward over a period of time, you would want to be sure that any changes observed reflect real changes in the patient group rather than inaccuracies inherent in the scale, or changes on a dimension that you do not intend to measure. Good reliability and validity ratings are rare and it should not be assumed that simply because a scale is widely used or referred to in professional journals that it is reliable or valid. For example, Hall (1980) reviewed 29 rating scales used in long-stay settings and only four met minimal criteria regarding scale construction. A word of caution is also required concerning the over-reliance that is sometimes placed on such scales. Whilst a number have reasonable validity, no rating scale has been developed which is able accurately to predict the resettlement needs of an individual. The important point is that, within the constraints of time and money available, a combination of methods is much more effective than any single measure.

### Assessment for planning purposes

In planning for the transition from hospital to community, particularly when a large number of patients is involved, there is a requirement to collect some basic quantitative data. This should include information on the size of the population, their age, sex, ethnicity, length of hospitalisation, diagnosis, chronic physical disabilities and some rating of dependency. Although relatively easy to collect, a problem remains about what to do with the information. There are a number of norms available for service provision (for example within the 1975 White Paper publication *Better Services for the Mentally Ill* (DHSS, 1975)), but these norms are a crude basis for any service plan. As needs vary so widely between localities, they can provide, at best, a baseline against which the minimum standards for the service can be set. The information can also provide a basis on which the initial calculation of service costs can be made. In addition, it allows for some basic monitoring of the population, and, more importantly, the changing patterns of service use over the transitional period. Two important variables are the build up of new long-stay patients and the mortality rate among the old long-stay hospital population, both of which will have a considerable impact on service reprovision. (See Shepherd (1988b) for examples of the use of this kind of information.)

Adding to this basic information brings a choice point in the assessment process. Invariably more detailed planning is concerned with specifying the need for residential accommodation, day services (often coming a poor second to residential services in the rush to reprovide 'beds') and support services. In obtaining the necessary information for more refined service development is it better to have a system that is based on some form of survey, or alternatively on detailed individual assessments? A number of factors affect this choice, including the merits of the measures available and the resources available for completion of the assessments. These resources include the staff available to undertake the exercise, the skills of this staff group, the time constraints on the exercise and the attitude within the institution to the closure process. Some methods demand much more cooperation from staff than others and their lack of cooperation could effectively sabotage the exercise.

There are a number of assessment methods which lend themselves to a survey procedure. Broadly there are two different methodologies. The first involves the use of some form of direct rating of patient behaviour, the second a rating by staff of patient need. In the former case, with the use of a scale like REHAB (Baker and Hall, 1983) it is possible to obtain, with appropriate training, a reasonable degree of reliability and the scale is relatively simple to use. However, in common with a number on similar scales, REHAB gives a rather oversimplified rating of need (it groups patients into one of three dependency categories) and the problem remains as to how to relate these categories or total scores to potential community-based services. Alternatively, the other method asks direct questions of staff on the types of service needed by patients. An example of this kind of scale is the Community Placement Questionnaire (Clifford, 1987). Such methods have the advantage that by varying the content of the questionnaire, they can be tailored to suit local needs. However, they tend to lack the reliability of more standardised scales like REHAB and have the potential drawback that they rely on ratings made by staff, who may have little or no experience of services outside hospital. Staff problems in making accurate ratings are further complicated by the situation-specificity of behaviour. Ultimately, local circumstances will dictate the methods chosen. It is important to remember to avoid over-reliance on any one method and to use any opportunities available to review and refine the information obtained.

Surveys provide information which lends itself to easy integration into the planning process. If done well they can also be a useful way to involve direct care staff in the planning process and so help them to develop a sense of ownership (this is very much helped by appropriate feedback to all involved). They can also bring planners and managers into more direct contact with service providers and users than they would otherwise be. As a consequence they can help to dispel myths held by various groups about the hospital population. The process of analysing the information, which is inherent in a survey, can highlight issues that otherwise might not be apparent and also allows for comparisons to be made with other similar populations. On the negative side, they are time consuming and, if, for example, you are to survey 750 people in a reasonable time, expensive on other resources as well as time. There is also a danger that inappropriately selected instruments will fail to reflect important characteristics of the hospital population and thereby mislead the planning process. Finally, there is the question of how effective the information collected will be in determining the nature and content of future plans in the face of many other pressures on the planning process.

There is a second methodology which explicitly rejects the broad survey. It is based on the view that all planning assessments must be rooted in individual need, based on a full and sensitive understanding of each individual which can only develop through the relationship between the 'planner' and the individual. One of the best known examples of this methodology is the *Getting to Know You* assessment (Brost and Johnson, 1982). Kingsley and Towell (1988) describe a number of interesting ways in which this methodology has been used, in isolation or in combination with other tools, to develop the planning process. It is probably best suited to a situation where planning can proceed in a slow, staged manner. It does not lend itself easily to the collection of a large volume of information and its main value probably lies in the refinement of existing plans.

## Assessing the individual

So far the discussion has concentrated on the collection of information for service planning and little has been said directly about the detail of individual assessment. However, much of what has been said above applies equally to detailed assessment of the individual. Indeed an assessment for planning purposes may be seen as the starting point of a more detailed individual assessment. Standardised scales have a part to play, as do structured interviews or systems such as *Getting to Know You* but there is no substitute for real experience of an individual's performance in a range of appropriate settings. The basic elements of an assesment are set out below:

1  An interview(s) with the patient which puts particular emphasis on the expressed needs of the patient.
2  An interview(s) with the patient's carers. This could involve a range of people including staff, relatives and advocates.
3  A review of relevant documentation regarding the patient.
4  The optional use of a wide range of available rating scales looking at, for example, challenging behaviours, daily living skills, needs for night time support.
5  Real opportunities to experience, over a substantial period of time, a range of different settings and demands inside and outside the hospital.

However, at the risk of repeating the message once too often, no single procedure will provide the definitive answer. Proper assessment is a long and complex buisness which involves developing a working alliance with the patient over many months, during which time many different options may need to be tried. The pace of this process should, as far as is possible, be determined by the patient's ability to contribute to the task.

## PREPARATION OF THE PATIENTS FOR THE MOVE

The detail of preparing patients for the move from a hospital that is closing is no different from much of the work that is done in the ordinary process of rehabilitation and resettlement. What is very different is the context that it takes place in and this imposes some particular constraints and presents some awkward challenges. This section will only provide the framework, details of individual work being discussed in more fully in Chapter 3.

There are a number of misconceptions that surround rehabilitation which can affect the process of patient preparation. Amongst the most damaging of these is the 'ladder model' of rehabilitation. This model assumes a steady progression through a series of stages, each stage characterised by increasing levels of competency and, at its worst, it requires an individual to succeed at each stage before leaving hospital. There are a number of problems with this model. First, it fails to understand the environment-specific nature of many problems encountered in rehabilitation. What this model sees as a gradual progression can in fact become a series of new challenges, often unrelated to the previous or future environments. Secondly, it is often based on an implicit link between successful rehabilitation and resettlement, success only really being achieved if some form of independent living arrangement is obtained. Thirdly, it contains the seeds of severe disappointment, for both staff and clients, because of the association of success with reaching a common end point. Fourthly, it can result in too great an emphasis being placed on training in a number of self-care skills, or the overcoming of problem behaviours at the expense of personal orientation to, or psychological preparation for, the move from hospital. Finally, because of the resources that are inevitably tied up in supporting such a structure, it often draws resources away from other areas, making it difficult to develop appropriate care plans elsewhere.

Another potential source of confusion is the matter of patient choice, particularly in relation to future residential provision. Great store is often set on offering patients a choice of accommodation. In reality choice is limited. This can be a result of constraints on resources or other policy decisions. It is important to remember that not all residents of long-stay hospitals that are to close wish to leave. Real choice can only be based on experience and many long-term mentally ill people with years of hospitalisation behind them have little or no experience on which to base their choices. In addition, a number of long-term mentally ill people, because of the fluctuating nature of their symptoms or associated cognitive deficits, may find thinking through such choices very difficult or at times impossible. Providing choice involves not only the offer of a range of services when an individual is to be discharged from hospital, but the establishment of a system which allows for the movement of people between community-based projects. It also requires the investment of considerable staff time and energy in aiding (perhaps through the use of advocates) and encouraging patients to make choices, particularly in a system where in the past choice has been often taken away from them. Whatever system is adopted it is likely that some disagreement will occur between service users and providers. Such disagreements should be noted and, where possible, explored; it is far healthier for them to be openly acknowledged than hidden.

Many hospitals in the process of closure are in a very poor state, both in terms of material resources (physical state of building, understaffing) and emotional resources (poor morale, lack of adequate staff support). This is, of course, often instrumental in pushing the hospital towards closure but there is a danger that staff involved in the closure programme only reinforce this poor state of affairs. This is most obviously seen in the denigration of the hospital and the overly critical attitude adopted by some staff, usually but not exclusively, from outside the hospital. Often there is a belief underpinning this critical approach which assumes that all that is wrong with most, if not all the patients, is that they have spent too long in a large mental hospital. Such an assumption is a denial of the disability and suffering that long-term mental illness brings for many people. A danger of this assumption, particularly as it is generally unspoken, is that it will lead to inadequate preparation and support for people leaving hospital. Unfortunately, when things do not work out the blame will usually be laid at the hospital's door. A particular problem with this implicit criticism is the effect it has on the direct care staff; put simply, being criticised and devalued does not make for a happy workforce. As Stanton and Schwartz (1954) demonstrated in their classic study of the mental hospital, problems within the staff group inevitably find expression in poorer patient care. It is one of the paradoxes of the current community care programme that is easier to close a good hospital that is functioning well than it is a bad one.

As with assessment there is no one method for the preparation of patients for the transition; what works in one setting may be quite inappropriate in another. There can be no prescriptions about what should be done. What follows are a series of questions for which answers need to be found before the start of any patient preparation work. Answers need to emerge from careful discussion and much valuable preparation work can be done by ensuring that as many people as possible have some involvement in the discussion.

1 Who needs to be involved – patients, user groups, direct care

staff, relatives, managers, planners from a range of agencies in both managing and receiving districts?

2 What structures or mechanisms have been established to bring these parties together – project groups or rehabilitation teams (to look at assessment methods; to coordinate the preparation of clients for a particular project); seminars and consultation (to disseminate ideas and become familiar with the principles on which the services are based, to discuss new strategies); information centres (to inform the patients, staff, relatives and the local community)?

3 What selection methods are to be used – will there need to be a survey, how will individual clients be involved; who should this involve (are more resources or training for existing staff required)?

4 Where and at what stage is preparation work going to be done – on the existing wards; on a specialist ward (does this require additional resources?); in the community-based project?

5 Is there an individualised system of care planning in operation? Does it take into account patient wishes and provide for their active involvement in the system? Is it geared to moving people into specific accommodation? Does it address the issue of psychological as well as practical preparation?

6 Who is responsible for the coordination of this work – at the hospital level is there an identified and accessible group or individual; at the ward/project level is there a group or individual, with sufficient authority, close enough to the ground to oversee the work; at the patient level is there a case coordination or key worker system in operation?

7 Who is going to carry out the agreed work – are staff going to be released from within the hospital (and if so will they have had time to become familiar with the projects and the locality as well as the patients)? Are staff going to be taken on early from the project (how will they be familiarised with the hospital and integrated with the work of existing staff)?

8 How will continuity of care be ensured over the transitional process – will staff move with patients, are locally-based support staff (other than the direct carers) involved prior to transfer?

9 Have the training needs of the staff been considered?

10 Has enough time been allowed (a useful rule of thumb seems

to be that projects take three times as long to establish as the orignal estimate!)?

## PREPARATION OF STAFF FOR THE MOVE

One reason behind the closure of the large mental hospitals is the chronic failure to recruit sufficient staff and, given demographic changes within the country (that is the drop in people of school-leaving age over the next twenty years), it is difficult to see any way in which the situation will improve. Given this fact it is surprising how neglected the staff of the large mental hospitals are both generally and, in particular, with regard to hospital closures. Indeed, many closure programmes could almost be characterised as conspiracies to avoid any contact or involvement with hospital staff. It is true that a number of staff in such services have acquired institutional practices and attitudes which can be detrimental to client care whether in a hospital or community setting. However, it is important to realise that these characteristics are not shared by all staff and even where they are present they are acquired and not innate. This means that they can change. Whilst many hospital closure programmes acknowledge the capacity for hospital staff to change there is sometimes a suggestion that this must be preceded by some kind of breast beating confession of the error of their previous ways; a mental health equivalent of the repudiation of past errors which Chinese intellectuals went through during the Maoist cultural revolution. But, as the Maoists discovered, such forced con-fessions are neither given willingly nor bring about lasting change; they foster resentment and counter-revolution.

How can this resentment and counter-revolution be avoided? First, the issue of job security needs to be addressed at an early stage in the transitional process. A workforce which feels itself wanted is much more likely to work for change than one which perceives itself to be unwanted. One of the most successful hospital closure programmes in the United Kingdom, that developed by Exeter Health Authority, began by offering all staff employment in its new community service if they wished. Secondly, there needs to be recognition of the skills and exper-ience of the large mental hospital staff. Hospital staff need to be confident of their experience and put their views forward rather than assume they will be ignored. All staff involved need to promote systems which ensure that staff views and experience are used constructively. For example, assessment systems or surveys which by-pass hospital staff are inevitably bound to create problems. Generating enthusiasm for community care on the part of hospital staff will not be achieved by 'indoctrination sessions' on the benefits of community care but is much more likely to stem from exposure to well run, effective community-based projects, preferably in the local area. Visiting such projects should be actively encouraged as part of staff's ordinary duties, with adequate time for feedback and discussion.

Whilst it is crucial to recognise the existing skills of hospital staff, the fact that further training and skills development may be required should not be ignored. Effective training can be a real incentive for staff in supporting any programme and is often seen as evidence of a real commitment. (The issue of training is taken up again in Chapter 4.) In considering the preparation of staff for the move careful thought also needs to be given to the personal and social support that the infrastructure of the large hospital provides. This operates in both formal and informal ways; for example in a formal sense many of the administrative tasks of ward management are dealt with by the hospital whereas this might well not be the case in an isolated community-based unit. At the informal level the regular contacts with colleagues in corridors, social clubs or other settings can provide valuable emotional support which can be hard to recreate in a more dispersed service. Addressing these issues through support and discussion groups at ward and unit level can be invaluable, particularly if backed up by a commitment to establish effective staff support systems in the community.

## PREPARATION OF THE COMMUNITY

In order to consider the preparation of the community it is useful to gain some understanding of what is meant by community. The word 'community' refers not any one grouping or location rather it is a loosely defined concept with almost as many meanings as it has usages. For the purpose of this book we need to consider several different communities which impinge on mental health services. There is the community of the hospital with its composite communities of staff and patients and the closely linked communities of the families and carers of staff and patients. There is also the much larger community of chronically mentally ill people and their carers who on occasion use the hospital's services. Then there are the 'political' communities of the local authorities and the health authorities (important to have allies here). Finally there are the communities as we more traditionally know them: the neighbourhood, the street, the village, and depending in part on where you see yourself living and what religious, ethnic group or other social category you belong to.

The preparation of the community is a complex business. Some of this complexity (families, staff, patients) will be dealt with elsewhere and so will not be discussed further. How easy other matters will be to deal with will be a product of the histories of the various communities. How committed local politicians are to community care can be very important; for example, when applying to a local authority for planning permission for a change of use of a building. A general point to be made here concerns the information that is made available to communities; there is a good deal of prejudice against mental illness in most communities. Well-presented information, perhaps in a creative collaboration with local media, accompanied with some real examples of success for ordinary people can do much to challenge prejudice. Better still, encouraging communities to take a real interest in the life of a hospital can help even more. Consultation can be a positive step and, in the case of planning permission, may be forced on services. Generally this is made much easier if allies can be identified in relevant communities who are sympathetic and have a position of some authority within the community. Offers of help from local voluntary groups or concerned individuals should not be ignored but, if appropriate, encouraged.

There is a view of community preparation which argues that there should be no more preparation of a community for the arrival of a mental health project than an ordinary citizen might make when moving house with regard to his or her new neighbours. Whilst such an approach has a certain logic it may be neither possible (because of planning permission or similar legislation) or desirable; prejudice does not go away by simply ignoring it. Integration, however limited it may be, takes time and energy and, generally, the sooner it is started the better. Given the extensive and often justified pessimism about communities' abilities to care it seems appropriate to finish with an example of a successful piece of community involvement. When a local Tenants Association based in Clerkenwell, Islington, heard of plans to close the large mental hospital that served their area they approached the local council and asked if they could be involved in the development of a locally-based residential project, preferably but not exclusively for people from the local neighbourhood. Their offer was well received by both local authority and health authority staff; accommodation was found in the area and a group, comprising professional staff and local residents, established. The group has had a central role in overseeing the development of the project. The project is now complete and nine people have moved into two houses in Clerkenwell, not an everyday occurrence but evidence that opportunities do exist and that communities can care.

*Chapter Three*

# WORKING WITH THE INDIVIDUAL

## INTRODUCTION

The individual must always be at the centre of any rehabilitation or treatment programme. This may seem so obvious as to be not worth stating, but where so many individuals or agencies may be involved in the care of an individual, it bears repeating on many occasions. For example, an individual's accomodation, the type of occupation taken up during the day, the skills that may need developing in community living, the state of their physical health or the monitoring of long-term psychotropic drugs can all be a part of a rehabilitation programme and involve a wide range of professionals. Clearly decisions in such areas cannot be made without the direct involvement of the individual concerned and achieving this requires well-established systems for the coordination and development of individual care packages.

The means by which these individual care packages are developed has been the subject of continual debate in the field of rehabilitation; much of it fed by a concern about access to resources. Indeed this concern has been at the centre of the recent White Paper *Caring for People* (DHSS, 1989). A range of methodologies has developed, the details of which have varied considerably. All good systems, however, can be said to contain the following elements:

1 An initial assessment
2 An action plan
3 A process of implementation
4 A system of evaluation

What follows is a discussion of each of the above areas, drawing when necessary on existing systems as examples. Individual care planning systems develop in response to particular circumstances and so it is unlikely that any one system will suit all circumstances without some refinement.

## THE INITIAL ASSESSMENT

The term initial assessment has been chosen to stress that assessment is a continual process that starts rather than finishes with the development of a rehabilitation programme. Some of the methods available for use in rehabilitation have already been described in Chapter 2. Many of the methodologies described there are applicable to the work discussed in this chapter but there are differences. The first and most important step in assessment is that there needs to be a relationship established between assessor(s) and the assessee, so that the nature and purpose of the assessment is understood. This relationship, if successfully established, can be the beginning of a partnership upon which much future work can be built. Where this cannot be achieved at the beginning there must be a commitment to work towards it. In some cases, for example in the relationship between patient and doctor, there may already be a substantial basis for this understanding along with a system for regulating such a relationship. However, whatever the circumstances, the purpose of the assessment should be spelt out as clearly as possible.

The second essential requirement is that the initial assessment provides an appropriate context which allows for the development of a framework on to which further information can be added as it emerges. This should be an automatic starting point for any assessment but it is surprising how often such information is missing. The basis for this context is a history of the individual's past and present life experience and also their experience of rehabilitative and other caring services. Often assessments are done on people who have long experience of rehabilitation services and it is therefore assumed that everyone is familiar with the past history or, worse still, that events which happened some years ago are no longer of relevance. Too many rehabilitation services, in their anxiety to help individuals, concentrate on a narrow skills or symptom-based approach to the exclusion of other factors. As a consequence important members of the individual's social network may be ignored. A well-taken psychiatric or social history can often be the appropriate way to provide the right context. Often where such information is available it can be rather stale, even where it has been regularly reviewed, and needs some form of refreshment. A new set of eyes cast over the information may help. Alternatively simply sitting down with the client and developing an account of an average day's activities, if possible in pictorial format, can enliven and inform the beginning of any assessment procedure.

A third important requirement is that assessment should concentrate on an individual's strengths as well as weaknesses. Excessive concentration on weaknessess (a disease to which the 'pathologically minded' health service worker is particularly susceptible) gives a distorted picture of an individual which can lead to undue pessimism from the start.

There are also a number of technical points concerning assessment which have already been covered in Chapter 2 but which nevertheless are worth re-emphasising. The reliability and validity of any formal assessment system must be borne in mind when considering that method. Even where reliability and validity are generally good, few scales have sufficient predictive validity to allow for their use as the sole instrument for the prediction of future community placement at the individual level. For example, a score below a certain level on the REHAB scale (Baker and Hall, 1983) should not be taken as proof that an individual cannot be placed in an independent living situation. Formal assessment systems do bring a major advantage with their concentration on objective measurement and this can be particularly useful in the assessment of change in an individual over the period of an intervention. Objective measures with clear descriptions of the frequency, duration and severity of a behaviour can be very useful in the assessment of anti-social behaviour, where individual staff opinion is often less than reliable. Assessments also need to be sensitive enough to measure change that may occur only very gradually and by small degrees. Assessment systems should seek therefore to measure attainable change and should not handicap progress by operating with too high a baseline (so that the individual's performance is always at the bottom of any scale) or too low a ceiling (so that the individual appears to make little progress).

Individual behaviour varies greatly from one setting to another. This is true of everyone but for those people who, by reason of illness or emotional difficulty, find learning and adapting to new situations difficult, it is doubly the case. The implications of this for assessment are clear. A complete assessment of individual need can only take place in those settings where the performance of the necessary behaviours to fulfil those needs takes place; the same of course is true when it comes to environments for the development of skills. However, where it is not possible to perform assessments in ideal settings then care must be taken to try and recreate these settings, e.g. assessing domestic skills in a kitchen of a rehabilitation unit that is on the household domestic scale rather than the institutional catering scale. Ignoring this can have serious consequences, with a failure of skills learned in one setting to transfer to a new setting (Shepherd, 1978). It should also be remembered that the environment is composed not only of the physical resources of a setting but also the services and people that live and work in it. These resources can have both a facilitating and inhibiting effect and must be taken into account.

Hall (1980) provides a very useful review of many existing standardised ratings in long-stay settings while the reviews of Anthony and Farkas (1982) and Wallace (1986) offer more extensive coverage of outcome and assessment methods for use in a range of rehabilitation settings. Whatever method is chosen, the information that is collected needs organising into a framework. Lavender and Watts (1984) provide one such framework. They begin by emphasising the importance of assessing physical health, an important issue given the high level of physical morbidity revealed by many surveys of long-term mentally ill people. Often an initial screening can be done by any member of the rehabilitation team with more specialist assessment being made available when required. Lavender and Watts also make the useful point that many people can function well in many settings despite quite severe psychological problems (e.g. persistent hallucinations) and therefore although assessment of such problems is important it should not be over-emphasised. The list below is a modification of the other areas described by Lavender and Watts.

*Self-care* - including personal hygiene, washing, laundry skills, personal health care, toileting, basic first aid.

*Home management skills* - including cooking, shopping, cleaning, simple household maintenance, budgeting, use of gas and electric services.

*Social skills and networks* - social interaction and role taking skills and the members of the individual's social network.

*Personal memory and orientation* - knowledge of names of family and friends, personal memories.

*Cognitive skills* - literacy, numeracy and problem-solving skills.

*Use of community facilities* - including public transport, social security, entertainments, day-time occupation, leisure facilities, social and health services.

In addition, it is important to consider any anti-social behaviour, paying attention not only to its frequency but also to its severity, duration, precipitants and to whom or what it is directed. Anti-social behaviour can on occasion become the central focus of an assessment and distract from much that is of equal or greater importance. However, given that it can be the major obstacle to successful community placement, it needs careful assessment. Watts and Lavender also discuss the important distinction between competence and performance. This is particularly important when considering any assessment data based on direct observation. In this context competence refers to the skills people have available to function in a particular role and performance refers to whether the person is able to deploy those skills in such a way as to attain a satisfactory level of functioning. A number of factors will have an impact on performance, including the perceived value, in personal and social terms, of performing certain functions. The individual's capacity for problem-solving skills will also greatly influence the attainment of satisfactory performance.

In an alternative model Anthony *et al.* (1981) describe the

41

process of diagnostic rehabilitation planning. This model starts with an exploration of what the client perceives to be the problem, what their understanding of the problem is and then provides a means of identifying the skills to be be acquired to overcome the problem. Once a problem has been identified, a rehabilitation goal is set and a detailed assessment then takes place. For the purposes of assessment Anthony *et al.* look at the interaction between environment and skills. The environment is sub-divided into three areas: the living environment (home, neighbourhood, and recreational facility), the learning environment (educational settings and training centres) and the work environment (competitive employment and sheltered work). Skills are classified into physical skills (for example, being well groomed, climbing stairs, being sexually active, eating nutritious food), emotional skills (for example, controlling temper, making friends, listening to others) and intellectual skills (for example, remembering directions, reading, cooking). A matrix is then constructed for each rehabilitation goal in which the interaction between environments and skills is set out (see Anthony *et al.*, 1981 for examples). From this matrix it is then possible to identify skills deficits which form the basis for training. Clients' strengths and competences are then used to enhance or achieve the desired goals.

## THE ACTION PLAN

The essential function of the action plan is to bring together the information that has been collected in the initial assessment. This requires the involvement of all those who have been involved in the assessment and those who will be involved in the implementation of the programme. It also requires the involvement of the individual who is the subject of the care plan, either directly or perhaps through some form of advocacy. The primary task of this review is to collate the information that is available and to arrive at an agreement on the extent of the client's need. Following on from this review the next task is to establish priorities for action. These priorities will usually be represented in the form of rehabilitation goals or objectives. In setting goals or objectives the distinction between long- and short-term goals should be borne in mind. When setting such goals the following guidelines should be considered.

1 Goals should be obtainable (within agreed timescales).
2 Goals should be measurable.
3 Goals should be established in agreement with the client.
4 Goals should be developed which:
    a) Acknowledge resource constraints (for example, are staff available?);
    b) Acknowledge environmental constraints (for example, are there opportunities for the client to carry out the task?).
5 Goals should be reviewed at agreed intervals

Essential to the process of review is that the information is recorded in a way which facilitates rather than impairs future reviews. Many services have developed elaborate systems for the recording of such information. Usually these are based around some form of formalised record-keeping system. In settings such as a hospital ward, appropriate use of problem-orientated medical records or the nursing process will suffice. However, such systems are not in use in many other settings, particularly where an individual is not resident in long-term care and this, along with the involvement of a wide range of agencies and other professionals, usually points to the establishment of a separate and specialised record system. The common elements of these systems is that they provide the following:

1 A method for the collation of information including:
    a) the identified need(s)
    b) the individual's strengths and weaknesses
    c) the agreed goals and their priorities
2 Agreed methods for achieving the goals
3 A method for identifying individuals who are:
    a) responsible for carrying out tasks
    b) responsible for monitoring progress
4 A method for ensuring the regular review of individuals.

Examples of such systems, in addition to the medical or nursing records mentioned above, are those of Anthony *et al.* (1981) described in the section on initial assessment, the range of computerised monitoring systems that has been developed for the coordination of community-based care (Martindale, 1987;

Whitehead, 1987) or the more elaborate organisational responses that have been developed around community support programmes (for example, Tressler and Goldman, 1982) or case management systems (for example, Kanter, 1989). Computerised systems are seductive and for most people have high face validity but they are no substitute for clear and careful planning. Many computerised registers established in the hope of 'solving' the problems of coordinating services for mentally disabled people have simply gathered dust. Computerised systems require considerable time to be devoted to the servicing and maintenance of data; usually this means more rather than fewer resources.

The completion of the initial assessment and the development of the plan of action cannot be divorced from the process of evaluation. The assessment tools used and the specification of clear objectives are the building blocks of any evaluation. To be effective, evaluation must be part of a continuing programme, short-term goals being subject to an almost continuous process of evaluation. At its most straightforward, effective evaluation can be simply a case of recording on a handwritten chart if a goal was achieved, how frequently and in what circumstances (number of prompts, setting, etc.). In the case of longer-term goals these may need a more formal structure, as provided, for example, by Goal Attainment Scaling (GAS) (Kiresuk and Sherman, 1968). The GAS provides for the specification of five levels of achievement for individual needs or problems ranging from least desirable outcome through to most desirable outcome. Pilling (1988a) provides an example of the use of this methodology in the evaluation of an individual intervention and its use in the evaluation of the treatment of a number of in-patients is provided by Guy and Moore (1982). Standardised rating scales provide an objective means of monitoring progress, provided the guidelines (outlined on p. 39) are followed. However, in the drive to demonstrate progress the views of the client must not be forgotten. Simply asking a client how they see progress can be a rewarding if salutary experience and rather more difficult than telling them how they have been progressing. There can be no substitute for careful listening to clients and their carers but an element of objectivity can be introduced into the area of client satisfaction by the use of structured interviews such as that developed by Lehman (1983).

## THE IMPLEMENTATION OF THE PLAN

Individual rehabilitation programmes cannot be developed in isolation from the environment in which an individual lives. Therefore, in considering any intervention, careful thought must be given to the level at which an intervention is made in the environment. Broadly speaking plans may be aimed at three different levels:

1 The development of a new service – for example, the successful placement of an individual in a new residential setting.
2 The development of an existing service – for example, a change to the content of an individual's programme in a day centre or an increase in the level of support a person receives in their own home.
3 The development of an individual – for example, teaching/ helping an individual to develop a new skill.

Clearly the distinctions drawn above are somewhat arbitrary and any successful intervention at one level may well demand action or have an impact at the other two levels. They do provide, nevertheless, a useful framework around which to structure interventions. In this section the concentration will be on the final level, that of individual development; new service developments and the development of existing services systems will be taken up later, particularly in Chapters 5 and 6.

Many people who receive rehabilitation services have long experience of personal failure and of being failed by services. Whatever the nature of their disabilities, they have usually been of considerable duration. This presents a major challenge to those working in rehabilitation. It involves walking a fine line between undue pessimism and unrealistic expectations. Put another way, it is about avoiding low expectations becoming self-fulfilling prophecies, whilst at the same time avoiding setting up people to fail. The steps for avoiding such problems include: first, setting goals which are attainable either through individual change or through changes in the environment; secondly, acknowledging that change will be slow and gradual; and thirdly, accepting that change will not persist unless equal thought and resources are available for the maintenance of the change as were available for the generation of the change. Often the implications of this are as important to consider for the staff as for the client; demoralisation of staff arising from unrealistic expectations of clients can have negative consequences. Staff need to be rewarded for their successes. They need to be helped to understand the importance of maintaining an individual's level of functioning and also supported in coping with the frustration of even the best worked-out plan going wrong. For many staff, working in rehabilitation involves not only the adjustment of expectations but also a considerable shift of focus, especially for those staff whose training and prior experience has been in the health or therapeutic fields. This shift involves a move away from placing prime importance on the control of symptoms or the management of behavioural difficulties, to one which gives equal emphasis to the development of new skills and the maintenance of social functioning.

## Individual interventions

The next section is devoted to a brief review of those individual rehabilitation and treatment approaches which are not covered in other chapters of the book. At the individual level the influence of the behavioural model has been most prominent. This is seen in the considerable emphasis placed on skills training by a number of authors (for example, Anthony *et al.*, 1981; Liberman, 1988). The influence of the behavioural methodology has already been seen in the discussion of assessment (see Bellack and Hersen, 1988 for further detail). A particular contribution is the insistence on clear objective criteria which allow for the development of clear action plans which in turn can be subjected to careful evaluation. It is beyond the scope of this book to describe in detail the full range of behavioural interventions, they have been well covered elsewhere (Matson, 1980; Hall, 1983; Liberman *et al.*, 1986).

In the development of individual skills the detailed behavioural techniques concerned with skills acquisition are discussed by Kazdin (1975) and Matson (1980). An area where there has been significant development over recent years has been social skills training. Liberman *et al.* (1986) present a comprehensive overview of work in this area, along with a conceptual model for the integration of social skills training into the wider field of rehabilitation. The model has four components; they are set out below.

1 Social schemata - which refers to the basic biological and psychological processes available to an individual in a learning situation. Schemata are the product of experience of past situations and abilities in a range of basic psychological functions, for example, memory or perception.
2 Social skills - which refers to the actual behaviours required of an individual in daily interaction with his enviroment.
3 Coping efforts - which refers to the attempts the individual makes to put social skills into practice.
4 Social competence - which refers to the impact these efforts have.

Social skills training, in Liberman *et al.*'s rather broad use of the term, focuses on both strengths and weaknesses (at the verbal and non-verbal levels) and aims to improve functioning through interventions in one or all of the above areas. They describe the application of social skills training to a variety of areas in rehabilitation, including problem-solving techniques, vocational rehabilitation and independent living skills. Further examples of the application of skills training are provided by Liberman (1988).

Skills training has enjoyed considerable success in recent years and it is one of the most widespread of interventions in rehabilitation. Unfortunately the enthusiasm for the method has not always been matched by empirical results. There are considerable problems with what Shepherd (1978) calls the generalisation problem and what Liberman *et al.* (1986) refer to as the transfer of skills from the training to the living environment. What both are referring to is the fact that skills training, and social skills training in particular, can be very situation-specific in its effects. The most important step that can be taken to overcome this problem is for training to take place in the setting where the skill is required. For example, the success of the behaviourally orientated models of family work in schizophrenia is no doubt in part due to the fact that the interventions take place with the whole family, often in the family home (Fallon *et al.*, 1984). Unfortunately it is not always possible to conduct social skills training (or any kind of skills training) in the right environment

47

and where this is the case Liberman *et al.* (1986) make the following suggestions.

1 Involve carers in the task of reinforcing skill improvements.
2 Use as many diverse training situations as possible.
3 Vary and 'loosen' the type of reinforcers used.
4 Blur contingencies and delay reinforcers where possible, particularly as the programmes progress.
5 Reinforce self-report and self-monitoring techniques; for example, through the development of 'homework' tasks.
6 Reinforce generalisation if and when it occurs.

An additional problem to be faced in any kind of individual intervention concerns the pace at which an intervention should progress. This is particularly the case with a person who has spent many years in relative isolation from intensive rehabilitation. If there is too much pressure at the beginning there is a real danger that the programme may result in a decrease rather than an increase in functioning. This problem can usually be overcome by careful monitoring and the prioritisation of one or two goals in the first instance. The importance of the relationship between staff and client should not be forgotten in the emphasis on skills training. A good trusting relationship between client and carer can provide the vital component which can help a client through a stressful period. Some authors argue that such relationships are central to the rehabilitation process, see for example the discussion of case management by Kanter (1989) which is covered in more detail in Chapter 6. However, there is a need for some caution here. There is evidence that the kind of intensive individual relationship characteristic of a pychotherapeutic relationship can be positively harmful to people with severe mental illness. In addition, people with long-term mental illness tend to be around rather longer than the staff that serve them and the experience of a frequently changing close relationship can again be very stressful. One solution to this problem is to enhance the social network of the client. Morin and Seidman (1986) describe a number of methods for improving the flexibility (the ability of the network to change its response as the individual's needs vary) and the stability of social networks. As there is considerable evidence, reviewed by Morin and Seidman, that effective networks can help to prevent relapse the import-ance of this work should not be underestimated.

Loss pervades the world of long-term mentally ill people. There are many examples, including the opportunities lost as a result of the disabling aspects of mental illness, the loss of community which affects those who leave the large mental hospitals after many years and the loss of friends and colleagues (the mortality rate amongst long-stay patients is much higher than for comparable age groupings). The psychological effects of such losses are well described by Parkes (1972). It is important that these losses are acknowledged by all working with long-term mentally ill people and opportunities provided for them to be discussed or dealt with in some way. Many individuals may find talking directly about such losses too difficult and so it may best be done through visits to former haunts, by opportunities to return to the hospital for visits if desired, or by building up a 'history book' of past experiences. Whatever method is chosen, the most important factor is that it should not be ignored.

### The role of medication

The subject of medication, particularly the use of long-acting major tranquillisers, remains a source of some controversy in psychiatric rehabilitation. There are four main areas on which concern centres and it is through addressing these areas that we can gain an understanding of the role of medication in the treatment of long-term mental illness. They are as follows:

1 The efficacy of psychotropic medication;
2 The methods of administration and prescribing;
3 The side effects of psychotropic medication;
4 The apparent reinforcement of an inappropriate medical model.

In addition to the above concerns, which all question in some way the use of psychotropic medication, there is the concern many professionals have with the poor levels of compliance with prescribed medication.

The efficacy of psychotropic medication
There is now a wide range of psychotropic medication available

49

for the treatment and amelioration of the symptoms of mental illness and distress. These have been well reviewed elsewhere and the reader should refer to texts such as Silverstone and Turner (1988) for a comprehensive overview. As the majority of people in rehabilitation services receiving medication will be taking some from of phenothiazine or similar major tranquilliser the discussion will focus on use of these drugs. The psychotropic properties of the phenothiazines were first noted in the early 1950s by a French surgeon who was investigating recovery from surgery. Since that time there has been a rapid development in the use and variety of the major tranquillisers. Fortunately, this has been paralleled by a growth of research into the efficacy of these drugs. What this research has clearly demonstrated is that in the short term major tranquillisers are effective in reducing and often eliminating the symptoms of mental illness such as hallucinations and delusions (Hirsch, 1982). What is less clear from the research is the long-term effectiveness of the phenothiazines and related drugs, particularly with regard to the disabling effects of long-term mental illness, for example, the negative symptoms of schizophrenia (Donaldson *et al.* 1983). Hogarty *et al.*, (1974) report a relapse rate of 48 per cent for people with schizophrenia who are on active medication as against a rate of 80 per cent for those taking a placebo. Other research into the effectiveness of phenothiazines has highlighted the importance of their interaction with other treament modalities. For example, the work of Vaughan and Leff (1976) demonstrated that certain family environments were associated with a high rate of relapse whether or not the family member with schizophrenia was not taking medication (see Chapter 7 for futher details). Therefore, it seems fair to conclude that major tranquillisers are an effective treatment, particularly for acute symptoms of mental illness, but that drug treatment alone is only partially effective for some people.

The method of administration and prescribing

Another criticism centres on the apparently routine prescription of drugs and in particular, of depot neuroleptics (usually in the form of a two- to four-weekly injection of a long-acting version of the drug). Indeed, Holloway (1988a) in a study of long-term mentally ill people using day services reported evidence of overrescribing and polypharmacy (the prescription of more than one drug – there is no evidence to suggest such prescribing is more effective (Wittlin, 1988)). Although there is some evidence to suggest that depot adminstration can lead to a reduction in relapse (Wittlin, 1988) it is becoming apparent that a more flexible and individualised approach to prescribing is necessary. Recent research has looked at the routine use of low dosages of depot medication and provides some support for its use in chronic schizophrenia (Manchanda and Hirsch, 1986). Others have looked at training both family members and professionals in the detection of the early signs of a relapse (Birchwood *et al.* 1989). Both methods offer potentially useful ways forward and would be helped if the very marked variations in individual response to medication were better understood (Baldessarini, 1983). The conclusion must be that the criticism has some validity, but the solution appears to be a much greater refinement in the use of psychotropic medication rather than its abandonment.

The side effects of medication

The side effects of the neuroleptics are well known; the most distressing being the oral-facial movements of tardive dyskinesia (which may affect around 15 to 20 per cent of people taking long-term medication). Other side effects include restlessness, sedation, hand tremor, muscular rigidity and increased sensitivity of the skin to sunlight. In total up to 40 per cent of individuals may suffer from one or more of these side effects. The side effects vary in their severity, duration and response to treatment. A significant factor is the idiosyncratic response of individuals to medication which makes it hard to predict who will be affected in what way by which drug. Also of importance is the evidence that the learning and maintenance of appropriate social functioning can be impaired by the use of long-term depot drugs as opposed to oral drug usage (Fallon *et al.*, 1978). To some extent side effects can be reduced either by the administration of anti-parkinsonian drugs such as Procyclidine or Orphenadrine or the use of low or intermittent dosages of phenothiazines (Wittlin, 1988). In addition to providing patients with as full an account of the risks involved as is possible, it is important that, especially where drugs are seen to be only partially effective, patients are encouraged, in consultation with a psychiatrist, to consider the negative consequences of the side effects against the positive benefits gained from continued drug treatment.

## The apparent reinforcement of the medical model

A major criticism of drug treatment is that it originates from and serves to reinforce a narrow 'medical model' view of treatment and rehabilitation. Whilst this can in some circumstances be true, where this is the case the medical model is not so much narrow as corrupt, viewing cure as the only really desirable outcome and, by implication, denigrating all other attempts at rehabilitation. An alternative and equally corrupt model proposes that all aspects of an individual's life should be the subject of medical scrutiny and control. (It should be remembered that it is not only doctors who can be guilty of the corruption of the medical model but also other professionals, carers and indeed clients, who, desperate for progress, may fall into the trap of a simplistic conceptualisation of individual need or rehabilitation.) Medical treatment is an important part of most rehabilitation programmes and should be based on a model of accurate diagnosis and appropriate treatment. A broad based multi-disciplinary, multi-agency model of rehabilitation is the most important corrective to the abuse of such a model.

The final area to be discussed concerns compliance with medication. Failure to comply with prescribed medication is often seen as a major factor in precipitating a relapse in symptoms of long-term mental illness. Although its significance may at times be overrated (alternative explanations often being dificult to identify), non-compliance remains a relatively easily identifiable cause of relapse and also one where the remedy is apparent if not always achievable. A number of factors are associated with non-compliance, including side effects, lack of information about the drugs prescribed, the method of administration, discrepancy in beliefs about the nature of the illness and its treatment between staff and patient and the rejection of the sick role. All the above factors are of importance, their relative weight being an idiosyncratic product of individual patient and service characteristics. Despite the individual nature of non-compliance there are a number of steps which can be taken which can help to reduce the level of non-compliance. The first stage in ensuring compliance is a willingness, on the part of staff, to listen to the patient's belief about his or her disorder. This means adopting a wider perspective than simply their views with regard to medication to include the patient's belief about the nature and cause of their illness. A difference of opinion between staff and patient may be unavoidable but if this is made explicit it offers the possibility of resolution or compromise. An individual's experience of previous drug treatments should be recognised and respected, particularly given the variation in response to drugs. The patient should also be positively encouraged to engage in the monitoring of their own symptoms (Birchwood *et al.*, 1989), perhaps through the use of diaries and other similar devices which may be aimed at detecting early relapse. The encouragement of self-medication programmes both in and outside hospital can help to identify or overcome some problems with compliance. The provision of specially numbered or dated wallets can aid in the accurate self-administration of medication.

## A SYSTEM OF EVALUATION

Throughout this chapter when discussing the initial assessment, the development and implementation of the plan and in reviewing the various techniques available, the importance of continuous evaluation has been stressed. Evaluation cannot be separated from these activities because if it is, the process of adjustment and review implicit in evaluation will be thwarted. Evaluation can be a threatening and anxiety-provoking experience for client and professional, particularly where progress is slow and difficult to achieve. Sharing responsibility for decision making with colleagues and clients can reduce the threat and anxiety and make evaluation a potentially valuable learning experience rather than a trial. The establishment of formal systems for review and evaluation, such as case reviews which make use of objective reports on achievements in relation to agreed goals, will help all concerned to make a proper contribution to the process of evaluation. Accepting the importance of evaluation means acknowledging failings and the prospect of more hard work ahead but it also offers the opportunity to celebrate success and so should not be ignored. In rehabilitation, where progress can be slow despite the input of considerable resources, it is vital for the morale of any service that its strengths and weaknesses are discussed. Evaluation of individual client's care is one important way in which this discussion can be facilitated.

# Chapter Four

# TEAMWORK

## INTRODUCTION

Rehabilitation is about teamwork and the people who comprise the team are the most important determinant of the quality of the service provided. It is clear in rehabilitation that no one individual or professional group has the necessary skills to meet the wide ranging needs of long-term mentally ill people. With few exceptions, this view is shared by most people working in the field of rehabilitation. Yet, despite the widespread agreement on the importance of teamwork, there is an equal level of agreement about the failure of teams to work, to function in an effective way, that brings the best out in team members. There are many reasons why teams do not work effectively. These include lack of clarity about policy, role confusion, problems with leadership, inappropriate skills mix and destructive processes in groups. Equally varied are the responses that may be required to resolve these problems. Effective teamwork requires understanding of the principles and practices of teamwork, including the reason for having teams at all! This chapter is concerned with the development and practice of effective teamwork and begins with a consideration of the purpose of team work.

## THE REASONS FOR TEAMWORK

Overtveit (1986) provides a summary of the reasons for developing teamwork models of care delivery. They include the coordination of care from a relevant group of professionals, the improvement of workload management, the establishment of common priorities and the provision of support to colleagues. In addition to those factors, the complexity of the task is such in rehabilitation that some form of teamwork is essential (Watts and Bennett, 1983b). Continuity of care is of vital importance in rehabilitation and it is unlikely that a single professional will be able to offer the continuity of care that a disabled person may require. So far, the reasons listed refer to the functions or purpose of teamwork. In addition, there is also evidence, dating back to the classic studies of the 'Hawthorne' effect, that working in groups (for that is what teams are) can improve the performance of the individual team member. Dwyer (1977) reviews the evidence for positive effect of teamworking.

It is important to temper this positive view of teamwork with a consideration of the potentially destructive aspects of group or team activity. These aspects of teamwork have been well summarised by Roberts (1980). They are worth restating as they provide a useful framework for considering some of the difficulties faced by many teams. Roberts, using a psycho-dynamic framework, lists the following destructive aspects of staff teams or groups:

1 Splitting – this can manifest itself in a number of ways. For example, an uneasy rivalry between different professionals or an unhealthy distance between staff and clients, usually accompanied by a dismissive attitude towards the clients. Both have their origin in a wish to see everything in black and white terms, as simply good or bad. Underlying this is an inability to adopt or contain attitudes or feelings which may be ambivalent or contradictory.

2 Subculturing – an inability in the group or team to acknowledge difficulties or disagreements. This can manifest itself in a team where the assessment and the treatment functions of a team appear to work well in their own terms but are perceived to be of little benefit by clients or other agencies. Such activity imposes considerable stress on staff as this apparent smooth functioning demands that a good deal is hidden or ignored.

3 Scapegoating – this occurs when an individual has blame heaped upon them in order to help the team avoid dealing with problems or difficulties shared by the whole team. Usually the

situation is complicated by the fact that most teams contain someone who, for personal reasons, becomes a willing volunteer for scapegoating.

4 Idealisation – this manifests itself where all the bad is located outside and all the team's difficulties are blamed on an external agent. In many teams this is usually an unsympathetic bureaucracy of some form. It helps to create the illusion that all is wonderful in the team and so inhibits proper critical examination of the team's work.

5 Splits in leadership – even in teams where there are designated leaders there are usually a number of people who take on leadership roles. The destructive potential of groups emerges when the rest of the team push those in leadership roles into increasingly polarised and acrimonious postions.

The processes described above can be part of the life any team; no team or group can claim total immunity. However, they are not inevitably destructive of good team functioning. The establishment, structure, policy and the setting in which the team works will help to determine what processes are at play. Many factors can counteract these destructive tendencies, including clear policies, effective management, good staff support and effective supervision. Perhaps the most important factor is that an opportunity is provided for staff members to reflect on their team's methods of working.

## THE STRUCTURE OF TEAMS

There is no one, correct way to structure a rehabilitation team. There are many models to choose from and the most important determinant of which model is chosen will be local circumstances. In this section a number of models will be described drawing on the work of Overtveit (1986), who distinguishes five types of teams:

*Profession Managed Informal Network* – individuals remain under the management of separate professional (or agency) heads and, although there is a common interest which gives rise to the meeting, there is no formal requirement on the team members to meet. Such a grouping may occur at a ward round where there is no formal leadership role but there are individuals, for example, the consultant in the case of the ward round, who have informal but nevertheless strong leadership roles.

*The Fully Managed Team* – all members of the team are managed by the team leader with, in some cases, outside professionals providing specific advice. Often such teams will be comprised of a single professional group, e.g. a Community Psychiatric Nurse Team, or alternatively a generic team where although individuals may be drawn from a range of professional backgrounds they will have the same roles and duties, e.g. as Rehabilitation Workers.

*Coordinated Team with Shared Management* – here each professional or agency head agrees on the appointment of a team coordinator who will share management responsibilities with those heads. Team coordinators have usually no authority over the profession-specific decisions of the individual team members.

*Core and Extended Team* – this covers two types of team. One where there is a core of team members managed by a team leader and with a group of attached professionals managed externally, and a second where both full- and part-time members of the team are managed by the team leader for all of the work they do associated with the team.

*Joint Accountability or Democratic Team* – here no one individual or agency has leadership responsibilities. Rather they are shared among all team members. Such teams can function well but this is inevitably where clear and strong informal leadership roles heve been agreed within the team, either through careful and often protracted negotiation or where there has been considerable shared work in the past and a 'natural' leader has emerged.

The choice of which model to adopt for a service is not easy and is made all the more difficult because, as Overtveit (1986) points out, there is little empirical evidence to support one model over another. What is as important as the team's management structure, is the way in which the team operates on a daily basis and here there is some empirical evidence to guide practice which will be discussed below.

## LEADERSHIP IN TEAMS

A central concern in all the above models is with the role of the team leader and great importance is attached to this role. Watts and Bennett (1983b), when discussing leadership in teams, point out that effective rehabilitation involves a number of individuals and agencies in the provision of a wide range of care. They argue that it is unreasonable to expect any one individual to have competence or expertise in all the relevant areas. Clearly there is a need for some overall coordination of the team's activity, but it follows from the complexity of the task that leadership of some form will need to be exercised by a range of team members. An important distinction is made between those leadership roles that are concerned with the management of team members and those concerned with the management of the tasks of the team. Teams cannot work effectively if the leadership arrangements for team members are not properly understood and their roles correspondingly developed. Clarity in this area will allow for effective management of the team's relationship to the external agencies. This is particularly important in community settings, as this aspect of the 'leadership role' was previously undertaken by the large mental hospital often in a covert way. Clifford (1988) describes the difficulties that can occur when the relationship of newly established community-based services to the various support agencies is not properly managed. In this area leaders have an important role in setting limits on the team's responsibilities and so protecting the team from being overburdened and rendered ineffective.

With regard to the internal operations of a team an important function of team leaders is to determine the nature of the decision-making process. The key to successful decision making in teams is that there is participation by all staff members. The extent of this participation will be determined by the skills, responsibilities and experience of the staff members, the nature of the task being considered and the demands of the external environment. As Watts and Bennett (1983b) point out, it used to be assumed that different tasks and circumstances demanded particular types of decision making. For example, firm centralised decision making where the situation is unclear and a more open, participative decision making where the situation is clear. However, Watts and Bennett argue that there is probably a requirement for both kinds of decision making in most situations. This does not mean that leaders will not be required to make unpopular decisions. Rather it is an argument against simplistic solutions where, in the face of uncertainty, 'tough mindedness' is seen as a virtue and not as an unfortunate necessity, perhaps arising from the system's failure adequately to anticipate or deal with a problem. Likert (1961) (see Table 4.1) provides a useful framework for understanding the various models of decision making. It describes both the style of decision making and also the characteristics of the team functioning associated with the various styles. In Likert's model the consequences of adopting differing decision-making models can be seen. Given what is known about the involvement of direct care staff in decision making from the work on quality of care (see Chapter 5), it is clear all teams should try to include an element of participation in their decision making.

## THE ROLES OF TEAM MEMBERS

A participative model of team decision making when combined with effective leadership can enable a team to overcome many of the problems that arise between team members. Role blurring is a particular problem in multi-professional teams and refers to the tendency for the duties and responsibilities of individual team members to overlap and become indistinct. Although a number of institutions positively encourage such blurring it is not without considerable problems and can lead to staff feeling deskilled and demoralised. Watts and Bennett (1983b) argue that it requires strong well-developed personalities among team members for it to work effectively. Where considerable role blurring is anticipated it may be more appropriate to establish a generic team with the same roles and responsibilities rather than a multi-professional team. Role blurring can be a particular problem in rehabilitation where a number of tasks require no particular professional expertise and may indeed be experienced as quite onerous by team members. In such cases it is important that all team members take a share of the load. It can be a valuable learning experience; a lot can be learned about stress and stigmatisation sitting in a Benefit Office for the afternoon.

*Table 4.1* Decision making in teams

| Style | Characteristics | | |
|---|---|---|---|
| | a At what level are decisions formally made? | b How adequate and accurate is the information available? | c To what extent are decision makers aware of problems e.g. at lower level? |
| System I Exploitative Authoritative | Bulk of decision 'at top' | Partial and often inaccurate informaton available | Often unaware or only partially aware |
| System II Benevolent Authoritative | Policy at top, many decisions within prescribed framework made at lower levels | Moderately adequate and accurate information | Aware of some, unsure of others |
| System III Consultative | Broad policy and general decisions at top, more specific decisions at lower levels | Reasonably adequate and accurate information | Moderately aware of problems |
| System III Consultative | Broad policy and general decisions at top, more specific decisions at lower levels | Reasonably adequate and accurate information | Moderately aware of problems |
| System IV Participative | Decision making widely done throughout team | Relatively complete and accurate information | Generally quite well aware |

Such activities can lead to a better appreciation of the roles and difficulties faced both by other staff members and clients.

In addition to those activities which it is reasonable to expect individual team members to share, there are a number which are specific to individual team members. This can be because of a particular professional training or responsibility, for example, a psychiatrist who prescribes medication or a social worker who applies for a formal admission under the Mental Health Act. Alternatively it can arise as a result of skills acquired as part of some specialist training, for example as a family therapist, which may be independent of a core professional training. The import-ant point is that these differences will need to be reflected in the working of the team. A major difficulty faced by teams, particu-larly democratic or non-hierarchical teams, is the denial of any difference between members. Taken to an extreme this can have a very disabling effect on a skilled multi-professional team with members feeling deskilled and under-valued. Professional trainings not only provide different skills but a particular perspective which is unique to that profession. Such perspectives, when held against those of other professional groups, encourage a broad conceptualisation of an individual's needs. Healthy team functioning depends on these contributions being both valued and encouraged. Earlier in the chapter, reference was made to the problems of attacks on the leaders, often motivated by envy. A similar problem occurs when team members become envious of the particular skills or responsibilities of each other. This may be overcome by first recognising and valuing the work of all team members and taking care not to award false premiums to certain activities (for example, psychotherapy) which only certain members of the team are allowed to perform. Secondly, it can be countered by the appropriate involvement of all staff in the development of care plans and their method of delivery.

The problems that arise out of the difficulties described above can be formidable, not least because they often operate at unconscious levels. One solution to this problem that has gained in popularity recently has been the establishment of generic teams where professional differences are not recognised in the team's structure. Such a solution has become quite common in rehabilitation. It is hoped that such an approach will eliminate the difficulties described above. In many cases this is simply wishful thinking; there are occasions where generic teams can be effective, particularly where the team members are expected to spend much of their time on a number of key common tasks, for example the provision of a case management system. However, there is a danger, in teams which have a wide range of functions, that generic teams will run the serious risk of being composed of individuals who feel unskilled and lacking in direction, so perform ineffectively. Often the problems of generic teams are also compounded by the fact that although duties and responsibilities are common to all team members, terms and conditions of employment, including salary, are not. However, successful generic teams can provide an important pointer to the successful establishment of multi-professional teams. When successful they are characterised by well-defined roles, both in relation to each team member and also in relation to external agencies. Role clarification, which is not the opposite of role blurring, is often a key factor in ensuring effective team work. Role clarification allows for the successful articulation of the team's tasks. In discussions of team work much has been made of the promotion of team cohesiveness, but this approach can lead to a very insular kind of 'group think' and a better term may be coherence. Coherence refers to the elaboration of the tasks of the team in a manner which allows for the differentiation and development of the team's work.

In addition to the recognition of difference another way to resolve some of the problems of multi-disciplinary team working is through the structuring and organisation of the team's tasks. The case management model (see Chapter 6) is an increasingly popular way in which the tasks of a rehabilitation team are organised. However, to function effectively such systems require considerable development of the care delivery system which is usually beyond the influence of a clinical team. More often a 'key worker' system of some form is in operation, where individuals are charged with responsibility for the coordination of rehabilitation plans which have been agreed with the team. Such an approach has the clear advantages of having a designated individual who is responsible for coordination of the care and the involvement of a range of other professionals and agencies. It also provides a means by which members of the team can feel they have a role in determining the direction of the team's activities. Problems can arise, however, particularly in long-term care where the individual key worker not only coordinates but forms a more intensive, possibly therapeutic, relationship. This can sometimes result in a series of intense but short-lived relationships for clients which can be potentially damaging in their effects. It is important for the success of a key worker system that, while the responsibility of the key worker is central, all members of the team are accessible to clients in an appropriate way. There is also a requirement for good, accessible information about the activities of staff and clients.

## TEAM BUILDING

The chapter so far has examined some of the reasons for teamwork, the problems that may be encountered and some of the possible methods for the establishment and management of teams. However, successful teams are never created by following 'recipes' in textbooks; there is a process of team development which needs to be followed even if all the 'ingredients' are correct. Such a process is usually referred to as team building. What follows are some of the key factors to be considered in the process of team building.

## Size

Size has a crucial effect on how a team develops and is the limiting factor on whether or not a collection of individuals can be called a team in any meaningful way. In rehabilitation settings teams of six or eight are commonplace and this probably approaches the upper limit at which a team can function effectively as a single unit. Going beyond these numbers means thinking of sub-groupings within the team, a move which brings with it the potential for new problems. With teams of a fairly small size (three to four members) thought must be given to development of staff support, of dealing with the potential role conflicts and with ensuring that the team does not become too isolated from external influences. In larger teams the facilitation of information exchange is crucial and there is a much greater need for efficient, accessible and comprehensible record systems. Much of the discussion that follows will have some interplay with team size.

## Team philosophy

Throughout this book the importance of clear principles based on explicit values has been stressed as being central to the development of good rehabilitation practice. Given that teams are at the cutting edge of the service delivery, it is vital that they have a clear perception of the values and principles of the service. In relation to the team philosophy two tasks emerge. First, there is the development of an understanding of the basic values and philosophy of the team and secondly, there is the translation of this into the objectives for the team. In relation to these two tasks it is important that a balance is struck between the development of a shared vision for the team and the need to encourage and develop individual perspectives within the team. Another tension arises between the need for the team to develop some ownership of values and objectives of the team, perhaps playing a role in their refinement, and the responsibilities of management in keeping the team within parameters that are compatible with the overall direction of the service.

Dwyer (1977) argues that an essential component of successful team building is making the tensions described above as open and explicit as possible. If this is not done there is a danger that managers, in order to avoid a discussion or resolution of the tensions, may give the team a degree of autonomy which is incompatible with the demands placed on the team, only to return to an autocratic style of management later when the team steps out of line. It is essential that at an early stage of team building, managers and team members come together and discuss their respective responsibilities. Clear information on the history of the team's development and clarity about the wider context in which the team is working are an important part of such discussions. The development of shared philosophies takes time and it is important that team members have time to think these things through. Such thinking can be assisted by having real work experience alongside team development time. Intensive, month-long induction programmes with little associated real work experience can be very destructive to future team functioning.

### Operational policy

The operational policy helps to set out a number of key relationships both within and outside the team. Where one exists, it is important that during the process of team building team members are involved in reviewing the policy in detail, amending and elaborating it where appropriate. This serves to develop ownership of the policy, to clarify the functions of the team and to identify areas on which further team development work is necessary. Overtveit et al. (1988) identify a number of key areas which it is generally accepted should be covered in any operational policy. They include: team aims and client group(s) served, team functions and practices, team membership, team meetings and systems of accountability, referral procedures, assessment and allocation procedures, team members' roles, recording and monitoring systems, and staff support and development systems. Such a comprehensive list inevitably means that there will have to be some elaboration of the policy, particularly as the team gains in experience.

## Skills mix and the roles of team members

This issue has already been discussed in an earlier section. The roles of team members will in large part be determined by the tasks facing the team. Understanding these roles will be facilitated by having members of the team with the requisite skills to complete these tasks effectively. It is the clear responsibility of team management to ensure that the required skills are represented in the team. The determination of the appropriate skills mix should be based on a clear understanding of the operational policy. Too often teams are established to readily available formulas which are not related to the needs of the clients. A community mental health team designed to support long-term mentally ill people in their own homes cannot function properly without the skills of a competent psychiatrist. A unit for the rehabilitation of people with challenging behaviours cannot function without team members who have a sound knowledge and experience of behavioural interventions. In team building there needs to be an opportunity for team members, in as non-threatening a manner as possible, to explore their own competencies and acknowledge those of others. This can usually be best acheived through some kind of structured exercises and may be assisted by the use of an external consultant, particularly where the team is new to each other or there has been a history of difficulties. The South East Thames Regional Health Authority have produced a team exercise called *First Things First* (South East Thames Health Authority 1988) which provides a useful framework for discussing some of the above issues.

## Team leadership

The issues raised by team leadership have already been discussed and following Watts and Bennett (1983b) it is suggested that a number of leadership roles within the team should be developed. This can take time but, for the purpose of team building, it is important that this process is made as explicit as possible. It is also crucial that senior managers are involved in any discussions. However, prior to the allocation of leadership roles, which may in fact be the formalisation of 'natural' developments within the team, there needs to be a shared understanding of what the leadership functions within the team are. Common leadership roles include the internal organisation of the team, that is, making sure that the agreed policies of the team are carried out. Here, the duties of the leader may involve the monitoring of all team members' commitments. This could include the number of sessions worked by those with a part-time commitment or ensuring that agreed procedures for case coordination or record keeping are followed. This role is best performed by a designated coordinator, who may well be explicitly employed for that purpose in a team with shared management. It could be the team leader in the case of a fully managed team or the senior professional in a multi-disciplinary team, for example, the consultant psychiatrist in an in-patient setting. Another important leadership role concerns the relationship to management groups and other external agencies. This will involve negotiations about the demands placed by such agencies on the team, clarifying the demands the team can make on such agencies. Further leadership roles can develop around the primary tasks of the team and here there are opportunities for team members, other than formally designated leaders, to take on leadership roles. For example, in a residential unit for severely disturbed individuals the psychologist may take a leadership role in the development of behavioural programmes. Again, in such a unit the coordination of the therapeutic activities of the day may be the responsibility of the senior nurse, perhaps through the establishment and monitoring of a key worker system.

Team building, like so much in rehabilitation, is not a 'one off' exercise but needs to be a dynamic and continuing process. This demands skills of a team, in particular an ability to examine its own functioning which remains a prime indicator of a healthy organisation. Team building should, therefore, encourage this process of reflection as one of its central aims.

The discussion so far has concentrated on the newly

established team, but in many instances teams already exist or are in the process of modification when the need for some kind of team building is identified. Where this is the case then the issues identified above are just as important. However there needs to be a careful process of what Dwyer (1977) calls diagnosis before any team building is embarked on. This involves taking a careful history of the team, with respect shown for the solutions that the team may have developed, an identification of the points which require development and those which will permit development. Whatever the diagnosis and treatment, an element common to most programmes will be some form of training and it is to a consideration of training that we turn.

## STAFF TRAINING

The core training of most professionals is limited in the time devoted to psychiatric rehabilitation or to the care of other disabled groups. The problem this presents lies both in the lack of real experience of rehabilitation settings and of an appropriate theoretical framework for understanding the tasks of rehabilitation. The challenges presented to any training programme in rehabilitation are then considerable. Training is not a 'one off' activity, it must be continuous and properly resourced if it is to be effective. As Lavender and Sperlinger (1988) suggest, training should be based on the work setting and address not only the knowledge that staff are expected to acquire, but also staff attitudes and skills development. Training should reflect the philosophy and objectives of the service and be as concerned with the application of skills and knowledge as with their acquisition. The discussion of training that follows is concerned with the identification of training needs, the setting for training and the methods of training.

### The identification of training needs

If staff training is to be a continual process, there needs to be a system which continually assesses the requirements for training. The system needs to operate at both the level of the individual and that of the service or organisation. The starting point for much of this work can be an operational policy which should provide a clear guide to the kind of activities that are required of staff in order to meet the identified service needs. With the development of a new service this is usually a more straightforward procedure than with an existing service. Lavender and Sperlinger (1988) describe a process starting with an induction phase (that is orientation to the service, client group and setting). It is followed by an operational phase (that is, systems for ensuring the continuing development of staff, for example, supervision) and finishes with a review phase (that is, a commitment to review the outcome of training). A major challenge is maintaining the continuity of any training. The problems encountered are similar to those met when developing training needs in an existing service. It is probable that success in maintaining training programmes is dependent on the successful establishment of systems of individual supervision or support which feed through to the development of training programmes. The degree to which this is formalised, through the use of personal development plans agreed as the result of individual performance review or appraisal systems, will vary across services. The formalisation of such systems, however, has a number of advantages. When such a system is established it should be done with a clear commitment from management to support the system by providing adequate resources for the training needs identified. Individualised approaches also allow for proper 'tuning' of training programmes; far too often circumstances arise in which there is a slavish implementation of a training programme which everyone receives regardless of need. A balance must also be struck between the development of individuals and the needs of the service. Effective training programmes which promote individual development can have a positive impact on the retention of experienced staff.

### The setting for training

There is clear evidence that 'on the job' training is far more effective than taking people out of their work setting (Milne, 1985; Rogers *et al.*, 1986). Yet, there is also a danger that if staff are limited in their exposure to other services then institutionalised practices can develop. Once again, it is a case of getting the balance right. The balance is important because training is one of the most effective ways to bring about change in an organisation. Whatever the venue for training the organisation needs to be receptive to ideas and innovation. Backer *et al.* (1986) comment on the importance of organisations being receptive to new ideas for innovation (and that includes training) to be effective. They identify the following factors as being important: interpersonal contact with professional peers, outside consultation with an expert agency, persistent championing of innovation, and credibility of the training programme. A clear implication follows: training must be taken seriously and the creation of specialist training posts is one possible way to do this, particularly in larger organisations. In smaller organisations or teams, individuals may be given specific responsibilities for training as part of a wider role. Given the importance of the setting in ensuring effective training it is vital that some training takes place in a multi-disciplinary context. Discussions about multi-disciplinary working are never going to resolve all the problems of teamwork if they are only ever held in single profession groupings. However, there is merit in separate professional training because it helps to preserve the unique contribution of each profession. Effective professional supervision of work in a multi-disciplinary setting can go a long way to ensuring this.

## The methods of training

Training methods can broadly be divided into methods internal to a team or organisation and those which are external. The distinction is somewhat arbitrary but nevertheless it provides a useful structure. Some common methods of internal training include supervision of an individual's work, seminars and skills training. It is possible that all may be provided by other members of the team or parent organisation; equally, outside experts may be called on to provide specific training. It is probably important that a balance is maintained between the use of both groups of trainers. Too much reliance on outside experts can be deskilling for staff, whilst an exclusive reliance on insiders can lead to a rather insular approach, starved of innovation. Internal methods have the real advantage that they focus on training in the workplace. With more formalised skills-based training there are a

wide range of methodologies available, including live supervision, taking the role of co-therapist with a more experienced
colleague, the use of structured training manuals, and video or
audio feedback.

Externally-based courses share many of the techniques of
internally-based courses and many of the more successful of
them place considerable emphasis on the supervision of work in
an individual's own workplace. With the exception of those
courses which are aimed at attitude change such as PASS
(Wolfensberger and Glenn, 1973) external courses tend to concentrate on specialist skills development and can be either multi-
disciplinary or uni-disciplinary. Often they involve significant
input of time and money (that is if anything useful is to be
learned) and a major challenge is ensuring that there is generalisation of what is learned on the course to the workplace. This
is most effectively done if there is a clear plan about how this
will be acheived. The Family Care Training for Schizophrenia
(FACTS) developed by Ian Fallon and his colleagues in Buck-
inghamshire is an example of how this may be achieved. The
basic components involve the training of two senior and competent clinicians in the basics of family management by intensive workshops in Buckingham, followed by detailed supervision over a six-month period of family work in the service of
origin. The two clincians in collaboration with FACTS staff
then train up to 12 colleagues in the service; the clinicians
taking on a supervisory role in relation to their colleagues.
Rogers *et al.* (1986) report an evaluation of a similar 'training
the trainers' model aimed at improving psychiatric rehabilitation skills in a number of centres in the United States. They
describe some limited success and there is a useful discussion of
the strengths and weaknesses of their scheme. External training
does not always need to be provided by outside agencies specifically established for the purpose. For example, a service involved
in establishing a new unit based on an innovative unit elsewhere
would be well advised to send some or all of its staff on
secondment to that unit. In the short term it can be expensive on
resources but it can save considerably in the long term. Much
more can be learned from spending two to four weeks in a unit
than can ever be picked up in an afternoon's visit.

Training is one of the most powerful tools available to ensure service quality. It can help overcome some of the teamwork problems that were described at the beginning of this chapter. No rehabilitation service can claim to be functioning effectively if it has not got a staff training programme.

*Chapter Five*

# RESIDENTIAL SERVICES

## INTRODUCTION

Discussion about community care has mainly focused on the reprovision of non-hospital residential services. There has been comparatively little discussion of the future role of the hospital in a community-based, as opposed to a hospital-based, service. However, the hospital will have a key role in community-based mental health services for the forseeable future. There are serious consequences of this neglect of hospital services, from lack of provision for the most disabled to considerable adverse publicity for services overall. In the United States, it has resulted in leading authorities calling for a halt to the process of deinstitutionalisation (Lamb, 1988). Hospitals will continue to be important for a number of reasons. Their function includes the continued provision of specialist hospital or hospital-like services for a small but significant percentage of people. Many people successfully resettled into the community will also require periods of inpatient care due to exacerbations of their symptoms. In stressing the importance of the hospital, the aim is not to assert the primacy of the hospital in community care, but rather to emphasise that hospital care has an important role to play in the provision of community mental health services.

## THE PLACE OF THE HOSPITAL IN A COMMUNITY SERVICE

Despite the considerable reduction in hospital beds in the last thirty years, approximately 70,000 people remain resident in large mental hospitals (Garety, 1988). It is probable that a large number of mentally ill people will still be in the large hospitals until well into the next century. In addition to this group, a large number of long-term mentally people will continue to be admitted for periods of acute in-patient treatment. Two aspects of hospital care need to be considered when discussing hospital based rehabilitation services. They are services provided by the large mental hospitals and the use of hospital services by long-term mentally ill people in established community services.

## The hospital as a rehabilitation resource

Community care does not end with an admission to hospital. Indeed, at the present time, it is the place where community care begins for most long-term mentally ill people. Hospital admission remains one of the main entry routes into the specialist residential and support services available to long-term mentally ill people. Furthermore, it is clear from a number of hospital closure programmes in the United Kingdom that the more effective the rehabilitation services of a hospital are, the easier it is to establish effective community-based services.

Since the seminal work of Wing and Brown (1970) it has been accepted that the environment of the hospital ward can have a major effect on the well-being of patients. Wing and Brown, in a careful longitudinal study, demonstrated that the availability of structured activity and the nature of staff–patient interaction had a significant impact on the clinical state of individual patients. Further work in this area, much influenced by Goffman (1961), has attempted to describe and understand better what constitutes good quality care. Lavender (1985) has summarised the relevant aspects of the long-stay hospital environment as follows:

1 *The resources* – including the staff, the physical environment and the financial position.
2 *The treatment practices* – including both psychological and physical treatment practices.
3 *Client management practices* – including opportunities for autonomy, staff–client segregation, and restrictive practices.
4 *Contact with the community* – including contacts both to and from the community.

5 *Staff-client interactions* - including both the quality and the quantity of such interactions.

### The resources

The physical fabric of many of the large mental hospitals make the resource issue a prominent one. It has been addressed in a number of government reports, most notably the Nodder Report (DHSS, 1979). The importance of appropriate physical environments cannot be over-emphasised and major expenditure of resources can be spent on obtaining them. Paul and Lentz (1977) in their comparative study of hospital rehabilitation environments offer numerous examples of the work required to secure and maintain appropriate environments and the financial resources entailed in doing so. Physical environments can be designed in ways which either facilitate or work against improvements in quality of care, from seating arrangements through to the physical appearance of the building (Shepherd, 1984). A particular problem with the hospital environment, as a rehabilitation resource, is the considerable difference between it and settings into which individuals may resettle. The implications of this for rehabilitation work have already been discussed in Chapter 3.

The poverty of the physical environment of hospitals is all too often matched by the poverty of the staffing complement. The empirical evidence with regard to staff–patient ratios points to clear deterioration in care when staffing falls below certain levels. However, simply increasing staffing ratios above a necessary minimum does not guarantee improvements in the quality of care (King *et al.*, 1971; Raynes *et al.*, 1979).

### Treatment practices

There is clear evidence that individualised programmes based on clear goals offer the most effective framework for rehabilitation (Liberman, 1988). Such a framework was described in Chapter 3. In addition to the establishment of systems which encourage the development of individual planning systems, it is important to guard against the blanket adoption of particular therapeutic strategies. For example, a milieu therapy programme which demands regular attendance at an analytical psychotherapeutic group for all mentally ill residents of a ward is unlikely to be beneficial (Talbot and Glick, 1986). Another important dimension of treatment practices is their comprehensiveness. It is important that the full range of an individual's needs is considered and that undue consideration is not given to particular problems (psychiatric symptoms are a favourite in any hospital setting). It is difficult to specify what particular aspects of a goal-orientated strategy are therapeutic, but it has been suggested (Hall, 1983) that the regular monitoring of staff implicit in such a system is the most important factor. Treatment practices should also include careful consideration of the medical treatment, in particular, that of psychotropic medication. Although there may be an over-reliance on drugs in some settings (Holloway, 1988a), there are settings where the monitoring and review of medication falls below what is acceptable.

Another important contribution to the treatment or rehabilitation function of the hospital is the provision of special environments for intensive rehabilitation. The most well-known example of this is the token economy (Allyon and Azrin, 1968), which has been the subject of considerable research and evaluation. Token economies are essentially carefully managed environments which allow for detailed behavioural analysis, intervention and monitoring. Achievements by clients are rewarded when identified goals are reached, the reward usually being some form of token which is given immediately and which can at a later time be exchanged for goods and privileges. The 1960s and early 1970s saw a tremendous growth of interest in token economies but recent years have seen a decline in both interest and numbers of units. In addition, there has been some modification of the original model with more emphasis being placed on the social climate of the units (Hall, 1983).

Paul and Lentz (1977) in their well-designed, comparative study of a social learning environment (a modified version of the token economy model), with traditional hospital and social milieu environments, were able to demonstrate the superiority of the social learning model. The emphasis in the social learning environment was not solely on the individual behavioural programmes but also on the importance of interpersonal communication, the status of patients and the importance of shared activites on the ward. Paul and Lentz demonstrated that the social learning environment was superior to both other models in increasing patients' adaptive functioning (for example, social skills and self-care skills) as well as decreasing bizarre behaviours. The use of psychotropic medication also decreased and there was an increase in discharge rates with consequent successful maintenance of community tenure. Hall *et al.* (1977), in a smaller scale study, were able to demonstrate improvements of considerable duarability. They compared groups of patients who were provided with either contingent (that is dependent on successful achievement of a goal) or non-contingent tokens, but who both received contingent social reinforcement. In the group with contingent tokens there was a slightly more rapid rate of improvement, but by the end of the study both groups showed equal degrees of improvement. This suggests that the effectiveness of token economies lies not in the tokens themselves, but in their impact on staff–patient interactions.

Despite the positive evidence described above, token economies presently exist only in modifed or diluted forms in some large mental hospitals and in a 'purer' form in a few specialist services. Projects such as those described by Paul and Lentz (1977) or Hall *et al.* (1977) are by their nature (research staff, enthusiasm, guaranteed levels of resources), and with the accompanying interest that this generates, untypical of the average large mental hospital where morale, staffing and resource levels are always threatening to drop to unmanageable levels. In addition, there is the generalisation problem (see Chapter 3) which may be encountered when an individual moves from the unit. This problem can be overcome, to some extent, by careful selection of individuals and the provision of maintenance programmes (Woods *et al.*, 1984). Clearly the failure to replicate the success of the above studies can be a demoralising experience for staff but if unrealistic expectations are avoided then these studies point the way for the integration of behavioural methodologies into rehabilitation work in residential settings.

Client management practices and their impact on staff–client interaction

Staff remain the most vital resource of any rehabilitation programme and it is through their interactions with clients that some of the major therapeutic and rehabilitative effects of any programme are transmitted. Therefore, it follows that the identification and development of those practices which promote the more effective use of these interactions will be vital to the success of any programme. As was mentioned earlier Goffman (1961) has exerted a considerable influence here. In particular the work of Tizard and his colleagues, (King *et al.*, 1971; Raynes *et al.*, 1979) who operationalised Goffman's concepts and demonstrated their utility in furthering the understanding of quality of care, has been very important. This work and its applications are discussed in detail by Lavender (1985) and Shepherd (1984) and only an outline will be provided here. Typically such work identifies three dimensions of the care enviroment:

*Autonomy–Restrictiveness* – the degree of client choice about the activities in which they engage, for example, meal times, getting out of bed, leaving the setting, having visitors.

*Personalisation–Depersonalisation* – the degree to which clients have their own posseessions, the amount of privacy afforded to clients and the recognition of personal events such as birthday.

*Staff/Client Integration–Segregation* – the degree to which the staff and clients operate in different spheres, e.g. the wearing of uniforms, distinctions at meal times. The way in which behaviour is explained, e.g. 'he had an aggressive outburst' rather than 'he was angry because . . .'

The empirical studies of Tizard and his colleagues have shown that environments which are at the positive end of the above dimensions (which they referred to as management practices) are characterised by a number of common features. These include significant opportunities for direct care and for other junior staff to have some autonomy in decision making within a unit. Such positively rated or client-orientated settings are also characterised by the involvement of senior staff in the direct care of clients. In this respect senior staff can be seen as carriers of the culture of the unit, involving all staff members in an appropriate way in decision making and where necessary modelling good practice. As it is clear that it is the quality not the quantity of staff–client interaction that is important, it is comforting to know that these management practices are associated with better quality staff–client interaction. Practices which are rated positively on the

above dimensions are associated with more respectful and positively orientated staff–client interactions. Shepherd (1984), drawing on a range of research and clinical findings, identifies a
number of factors which he considers are central to good staff–
client interaction. They include clear and high expectations of
clients. Feedback should also be clear, positive and related to the
performance of agreed tasks. It helps if all this is done in a
sensitive and socially approving manner.

## Contact with the community

Hospitals have a special responsibility to maintain contact with
the communities they serve. Isolation from family and the wider
community can significantly impair resettlement and the
development of appropriate support systems outside of hospital
(Morin and Seidman, 1986). Community contact should be a
'two-way traffic' with individuals spending time in their communities as well as receiving visitors. As was discussed in Chapter 3,
effective maintenance of the skills developed in a rehabilitation
programme is much facilitated by training in appropriate
environments and basing as much of the training as is feasible in
an individual's natural environments is important. The 'traffic
flow' should include not only patients but also staff who should
familarise themselves with the community which they serve.

Many of the good care practices described above are common to
a range of services which employ a multitude of different
theoretical models (Lavender, 1985). However, it is clear from the
above discussion that some rehabilitation programmes are more
effective than others. Menzies (1960) has described the defensive
strategies which staff develop to avoid the difficult emotions that
arise in their work and which have negative consequences for
patient care. She argues that careful attention should be paid to
the support and training of staff, so that proper systems for the
management of staff anxieties can be developed. It may well be
that the therapeutic effect of a particular regime comes as much
from the way in which it supports and guides the staff in their
interactions with residents as in its underlying theoretical sound-
ness, different staff and different clients needing different models
for working together, if progress is to be achieved and maintained. Quality of care is not a uni-dimensional concept, it is
multi-faceted and there are occasions where some elements of the

concept are in contradiction. For example, the requirements of a carefully developed individual plan which stresses structure and containment may conflict with the unit's commitment to developing individual autonomy. In such circumstances, the function of a particular theoretical model will be to provide a framework for the understanding and management of that conflict. This should help prevent the anxiety generated from obstructing the achievement of the individual's goals.

## The treatment role of the hospital

Whilst it can be argued that the long-term rehabilitation role of the hospital will continue to decline, perhaps to the point where only a few specialist services remain within the hospital orbit, few would argue that there will be no requirement for some form of acute in-patient care for the long-term mentally ill. This is not an argument for the retention of the large mental hospital but rather an acknowledgment of the need for in-patient care and a recognition of the need for clarity about the purpose and function of such services for long-term mentally ill people. Talbot and Glick (1986) have set out the purpose of such treatment and provide some guidance on the indications and contra-indications for in-patient care.

They begin their discussion with a consideration of the deleterious effects of hospital admission, namely that it is costly, can encourage dependency and that by disturbing an often fragile social network can lead to a real drop off in social functioning which may take many months to recover. They also acknowledge that the continued, and at times, inappropriate, use of hospital beds rests on a number of factors including the comfortableness and safety that staff can draw from working in familiar ways and the calming effect it can have on a disturbed social network. In times of desperation it is often invested with false hopes by many people. Before considering the indications and contra-indications of hospital admission they briefly review the evaluative studies of in-patient care which clearly demonstrate no adavantage of increased length of stay for the chronically mentally ill. Indeed, these studies suggest there are considerable disadvantages for patients in prolonged stays in acute settings with an increased risk of rehospitalisation, a drop off in quality of life and a decrease in social functioning.

Talbot and Glick place the re-evaluation of an individual's diagnosis and treatment at the top of the list of indications for hospital admission. Often this will be associated with an increase in symptomatology, perhaps being linked to a risk of self-harm or harm to others, or to an increase in disturbed behaviour which it is not possible to contain in a non-hospital setting. There may also be a need for a period of detoxification or similar monitoring of a complex physical manifestation of a psychiatric disorder. Finally, a short period of respite care may be indicated to provide the necessary relief to enable long-term community tenure to be maintained. Contra-indications to hospital admission they list as: because nothing else works or a particular treatment regime has failed; to change an individual's character; to convince a patient to change their living situation; to impose treatment plans on unwilling patients and to shelter malingerers or those facing legal charges. They stress that whatever the reason for admission, there must be a clearly worked out and agreed plan before a hospital admission is made. Finally, they consider the small number of cases where there is a need for long-term hospitalisation. They do not argue for the retention of the large mental hospital, but rather for some of the functions that the large institution performed, including specialist forensic services.

## The need for asylum

There has been much debate about the need for asylum within community care (King's Fund, 1987). The debate, unfortunately, has led to more confusion than enlightenment. Two strands can be detected running through the recent calls for the provision of asylum. First, there is a call, often from groups representing service users, for the provision of places of safety or retreat which individuals with acute stress or exacerbations of long-term mental illnesses can use when required. In some cases such calls arise from criticism of the inadequacy of existing acute services and the best response is to develop more appropriate acute services. However, all these services do not need to be provided in a hospital setting and in this sense asylum has much in common with respite care. So far few services along these lines exist, and it is a development which will need careful local assessment. Secondly, there is a call for the retention of the asylum function of the large mental hospitals. This call is usually associated with professionals identified with the large hospitals and groups representing the carers of people with long-term mental illness. A major drive behind their concern is the fear that, with the disappearance of the large mental hospital, there will be a net loss of services. This is seen as having two consequences, an increased burden upon families and other carers and an increase in the number of homeless mentally disabled people. Both are real concerns, but as Zipple *et al.* (1987) argue such calls are themselves potentially problematic as they can quickly become corrupted into a call for the straightforward retention of the large hospital. The appropriate response is to address the legitimate concerns of carers and professionals, engaging carers from the beginning of the planning process (see Chapter 7) and targeting groups such as the homeless mentally disabled whose plight raises concern among professionals and public alike.

## COMMUNITY-BASED RESIDENTIAL SERVICES

The past thirty years have seen a rapid growth in the community-based residential care of the long-term mentally ill. Its origins lie in the recognition of the inappropriateness of the large mental hospital as a long-term residence for most mentally ill people. What the renewed drive towards community care has brought is a changing threshold for acceptance into community residences. As a result many more severely disabled people have been placed in the community. This move has happened despite the fact that there is little empirical evidence about the efficacy of community-based residential care (Budson, 1983; Garety, 1988). Much of the research in the area has been descriptive and is reviewed by Ryan (1979). It reveals a wide variation in the development of residential services, with occasional examples of well developed local services. The position in the United States is very similar. Carling and Ridgway (1989) describe a wide variation in service provision and models with a lack of clarity about the direction of services. Even where good services exist there are deficiencies; often what is lacking is a framework for understanding the various functions of residential care and the needs of the local population.

The primary function of a residential service should be to provide people with a home. This entails making a distinction between a person's need for housing and the other services that may be needed. (With very disabled people this becomes increasingly difficult to maintain as the necessary adaptations to the environment blur the distinction.) Flexibility in the provision of support services is of crucial importance, so that if an individual's need for support changes a number of options are available. These should include increasing support staff or adapting the physical environment and not only, as. is often the case, simply moving the individual. The service also needs to provide opportunities for people to move to different kinds of supported accommodation. Although much of the support required will be long-term in nature, residential services also need flexibility with regard to short-term support. This means that resources can be increased at times of crisis, for example, by the use of peripatetic nursing teams. It must also be remembered that need is not a uni-dimensional construct moving simply from high need (or high dependency) to low need (or low dependency) along which an individual can be placed and a judgement made about their residential care needs. Some individuals may function very well in most areas but as the result of a single behavioural problem require a high level of on-site support. Resident choice also presents a real challenge to service providers and systems should be developed to facilitate residents' movement between settings. Moving from hospital ward to supported accommodation which residents are encouraged to see as their homes brings new challenges. If individuals are to be encouraged to see these new settings as homes how much choice should they have about who will live in their new home? If they have a tenancy agreement should they have to give it up (for example, to move to more highly supported accommodation) on the advice of a mental health professional?

## THE RANGE OF COMMUNITY RESIDENTIAL
## ACCOMMODATION

The range of community-based residential services is great, moving from highly staffed hostel-wards, through a variety of shared and single person housing with 24-hour support to shared and single person accommodation with daily support or less. Adult fostering, supported board and lodging and support to individuals living with their families or other carers complete the list. Almost as extensive is the list of agencies which provide these services from the statutory and voluntary sectors through to the private organisation or individual. An overview of this range is provided by Garety (1988), along with a discussion of the methods for financing such services. What follows is a description of some of the key areas of residential services.

## The hostel-ward

The extent to which a community-based service succeeds can be measured by how effectively it caters for the most disabled of its clients. In Britain the favoured solution to meet the needs of such clients is the hostel-ward or hospital-hostel. A number of descriptions of such services have now been published (Wykes, 1982; Goldberg et al., 1985). Such units cater for some of the most disabled of the present hospital population. The units vary in size from around 10 to 20. They provide a high level of nursing staff on a 24-hour basis and are closely linked with existing hospital services. In the case of the Maudsley Hostel (Wykes, 1982) this means being sited on the edge of the hospital campus, in the case of Douglas House in Manchester (Goldberg et al., 1985) it means sharing common staff and support services whilst being situated away from the hospital site. The rehabilitation approach of the units is much influenced by the work of Tizard and others on management practices and the behavioural strategies of the token economies. There is, however, greater stress on individualised planning and on emotional and cognitive issues than is the case with token economies (Garety et al. 1988).

Such units clearly leave themselves open to the charge that they are mini-hospitals or institutions, and to an extent the criticism is valid. They reprovide several functions of the large hospital. They acknowledge the need for long-term residential care and the need for a sufficiently containing environment to provide adequate treatment and support for disturbances of mental state and behaviour. In doing so they replace important functions of the old mental hospital which no community-based service should be without. There are considerable problems in establishing such units on a small scale because of loss of economies of scale and the need to provide a large physical space which seems essential to the healthy functioning of such units. Nevertheless, the question of unit size (for example, would a unit of four people promote integration and reduce institutional practice?) and links with local hospital services is matter for further research. It should be remembered that the evidence so far accumulated suggests that size alone is no defence against institutional practice (King *et al.*, 1971; Segal and Moyles 1979). Cost is also a major factor when small units are very intensively staffed. Hostel-wards currently represent a cost-effective model of care in comparision to other intensively staffed units (Goldberg *et al.*, 1985). There is also evidence that for the new long-stay group of clients such units provide a significant improvement on the quality of life over that provided by an in-patient unit (Simpson *et al.*, 1989). Finally with regard to institutional practices, Garety and Morris (1984) demonstrated that a hostel-ward, not only had client-orientated practices, but seemed to promote them in its staff (that is, those staff who had worked longest in the unit had the most positive client orientation). This may well be related to the clear systems such units have established for the support and development of direct care staff.

The first hostel-ward was established at the Maudsley hospital to provide a long-term highly supported residence for a group of very disabled individuals. However, Garety *et al.* (1988) have shown these intial assumptions about the long-term needs of the individuals were too pessimistic. Of a group of 33 people admitted to the unit in the first ten years of its existence, 21 have been discharged and in all but three cases these discharges were planned. In the case of these planned discharges 69 per cent have remained resident in less highly supported settings in the community; set against this is a number of people who have returned to the unit or who have never left the unit. This valuable follow-up study demonstrates that the hostel-ward can have a positive rehabilitative and resettlement function. When developing such units the geographical location chosen will affect the type of client that the unit can accommodate. The desire to integrate is a strong and significant factor in locating all services in community bases. However, for a small but significant group of clients, such community bases can be disadvantageous. Some individuals act in ways which put either the general public or themselves at risk. Here, services based in, or closely associated, with hospitals have significant advantages. It is important that services do meet the needs of this group as they are not appropriately served in the long-term by acute psychiatric wards or specialist forensic services.

Wing and Furlong (1986) describe a development of the hostel-ward concept which involves the retention of part of a large hospital site and the development of what they refer to as a 'Haven'. The Haven is an elaborate core (see p. 94 for more on core and cluster models) of four or more units with on-site support services which relates to an extensive cluster of less supported accommodation. It represents an attempt to use the site of the old mental hospital and yet promote progressive care practices. The eventual success or failure of the Haven will probably depend on how effective it is in escaping from the institutional practices of the parent hospital.

### Group homes

Group homes represent a significant proportion of community-based residential services. They were some of the earliest residential services established in considerable numbers in the late 1950s and early 1960s. In these early years they were often unstaffed, support being provided by visiting staff from the statutory or voluntary sector. Although the group home continues to be the main stay of community-based provision, the range of support available to the residents has developed considerably in the past 15 years. This increased level of support is a result of individuals with increasing needs being discharged from hospital. Many newly established homes now have 24-hour nursing staffing reflecting the needs of residents for specialised support and rehabilitation. Such developments are to be encouraged as they represent a significant improvement over the large, 20 or more place hostel that is still considered to be an alternative to hospital placement in some areas. The evidence from the United States (Lamb, 1979; Nagy et al., 1988). is that such large units can easily recreate the institutional environment of a large mental hospital with negative effects on residents' social adjustment, especially if such hostels are isolated from other services, have limited staffing and lack an extensive staff support network.

In determining the size of homes some compromise will eventually be reached. The compromise will arise out of the tension between economies of scale and the advantages of providing for more individualised care and community integration both of which should be a consequence of smaller units. McAusland (1985), in his paper discussing models for the organisation of residential services proposes 3–4 residents per home as the ideal size. Cost limitations usually mean that a home of around 5–8 residents is usually the outcome, generally those units with a higher staffing ratio tend to have a greater number of residents.

A number of studies describing, and in a few cases evaluating, the provision of care in group homes have been conducted both in the United Kingdom and the United States (Apte, 1968; Ryan, 1979; Segal and Moyles, 1979; Pritlove, 1983). They have often concentrated on the management practices of the settings and, not surprisingly, they reveal a great variety in the quality of care available to residents. Ryan (1979) paints a mixed picture of what can be achieved in a group home setting with the quality of life, social networks developed by residents, and the degree of activity engaged in by residents varying greatly. There was some indication in his study that the degree of resident disability and the type of staffing and management practices have some influence on the quality of care provided. Pritlove (1983) commented on the changing population of the group homes with a suggestion that a younger, more disturbed group of indivduals was inadequately served by those settings which stressed a family living model with its consequent demands for socialising and shared activities in the house. One response to this problem is to provide for highly supported (up to and including 24-hour nursing support) individual accommodation (Carling and Ridgeway, 1989). Another alternative is to create more opportunities for individual autonomy within the group home. In the United States the position is further complicated by the fact that there is much greater local variation in both the planning and development of residential services and the services that support individuals in the community. Nagy *et al.* (1988) note that the more disabled are more vulnerable to the potentially debilitating effects of large size community residences. Units which operated on a for-profit basis served the more disabled less effectively than those operating on a non-profit basis. Another study in the United States (Linn *et al.*, 1985) demonstrated that movement to another hospital ward was preferable, when measured on a range of clinical outcome measures, to discharge to large for-profit community nursing homes. Cost was the only advantage the community nursing homes had. In contrast, Perkins *et al.* (1988), in the United Kingdom, report favourable outcomes for a group of long-stay patients placed in a range of private for-profit group homes. Studies of the effectiveness of small units (that is, less than eight residents) which provide for clients with a high degree of disability are required. The so far unpublished evidence from the evaluation of the government sponsored 'Care in the Community' initiative by the Personal and Social Research Services Unit (PSSRU) at the University of Kent suggests that such units have serious problems in managing challenging behaviours and that this can be a major reason for re-admission to hospital.

Some indication of the kind of activities demanded of staff in these new settings can be gained from an important study of community living reported by Stein and Test (1980). They looked at the effectiveness of a 'Training in Community Living Programme' which provided for structured individually-orientated rehabilitation and treatment programmes in non-hospital settings for individuals who otherwise would have been admitted to hospital. It was based on six key principles:

1 Programmes must assume responsibility for helping individuals obtain material resources such as food, clothing and medical care.
2 Community coping skills (e.g. use of transport, cooking, budgeting) are vital and should be taught *in vivo*.
3 Support to sustain motivation and problem-solving skills is vital.
4 Freedom from dependent relationships should be encouraged and supported through promoting successful community tenure.

5 Direct carers and other involved in the community support of individuals should be supported and educated.

6 Services should act assertively, for example, they should 'chase up' drop outs.

Stein and Test were able to demonstrate that their model was effective at improving social functioning and reducing hospital admission as well as bringing a number of cost improvements. The cessation of their programme after 14 months was accompanied by a marked drop off in adjustmemnt of the individuals in their study, emphasising the importance of sustained and continued support for long-term mentally ill people. The comprehensive and assertive nature of Stein and Test's programme has now been replicated in a number of different settings, for example, Hoult and Reynoulds (1984). One clear requirement of such a system is extensive and effective staff support and supervision.

### Individual residential services.

Many mentally disabled people live isolated, lonely existences and struggle to gain access to appropriate services or social contacts. For whatever reasons family and personal ties have been disrupted or broken through the course of their mental illness. The model developed by Stein and Test provides one method to meet the needs of this group but there are a number of other less intensive support models which can be used to guide practice. The CARE system (Martindale, 1987) developed at the Community Psychiatric Research Unit in Hackney, London is one such system. It provides a means for the identification of vulnerable or at-risk individuals, allocates a key worker to them and then establishes an individual treatment programme which is presented to the patient and other relevant carers in the form of a 'Homepack'. The 'Homepack' is an information pack which contains a list of all involved agencies and individuals, sources of emergency help, and information on current medication. The CARE system also promotes the use and involvement of 'a trusted person', perhaps a friend or relative, who is nominated by the client to act as an intermediary between the client and the key worker or other aspects of the service system.

89

In addition to those mentally disabled people who live in individual accommodation there are those who live in Adult Foster placements (alternatively called Adult Care or Family Placement). Although grouped under individual placements, a number of adult fostering schemes take more than one individual, the upper limit usually being three. This limit is set by current legislation regarding the registration of residential homes. Such schemes have the prime advantage of placing people in already established networks, with considerable scope for flexibilty around the support provided by statutory services to both carer and client. Such schemes also call for careful and continuous monitoring as the potential for abuse and manipulation is an ever present risk. Howatt *et al.* (1988) describe such a support and monitoring system where a series of regular support groups for carers was established along with a careful system for the assessment of potential carers. They stress the need for appropriate back-up care or respite care and the need for access to day and other support services. Linn *et al.* (1980) in a large scale evaluative study of adult fostering, report a generally favourable outcome. Good outcome was associated with smaller size of residency, fewer placements in any one setting and the presence of children. For people with schizophrenia, a high level of supervision by foster carers was associated with poor outcome as was intensive follow-up by social workers, however the reverse was true for people with non-schizophrenic disorders.

## Short stay services

The necessity to provide appropriate in-patient care for mentally ill people has already been covered. However, some long-term mentally ill people require access to short-term intensive rehabilitation services, usually for a period of between 6 to 18 months. Ryan (1979) describes the workings of short-stay services which are typically hostels managed by local authorities or voluntary bodies. The client group of such services is invariably mixed and the demands that they make of the service equally varied. Ryan noted the difficulty such settings had in dealing with some of the more common problems of mentally disabled people, e.g. social withdrawal, poor performance in a range of daily living activities and general under-activity. As a consequence he questioned the the rehabilitative potential of such settings, their strength lying in the provision of accommodation or a transitional base rather than as a setting for intensive rehabilitation. Ryan identified the lack of 'technical' interventions as a reason behind the difficulties experienced by many shorter stay hostels. (There is some evidence to suggest that modifications of the hostel-ward model discussed earlier can be effective and also provide a real alternative to hospital admission (Hyde *et al.*, 1987)). Whatever the method chosen it is vital that the rehabilitative work, however short-term, is not seen as finished when the individual leaves the unit. The career as a 'revolving door patient' begins for many people with the discharge from a successful period of treatment or rehabilitation which is then inadequately followed up. Many units providing short stay services are further handicapped by the lack of appropriate supported housing for their former residents. Too often mentally ill people are denied the opportunity to establish themselves in the community by being offered sub-standard accommodation which brings its own psychological stresses (Brown and Harris, 1978). On a more positive note, Budson and Jolley (1978) described a short-stay hostel which had considerable success in resettling individuals in independent accommodation. The success was in part attributed to the considerable emphasis placed on maintaining links with mental health services and the development of extended psychosocial networks.

## The homeless mentally ill person

The position of homeless mentally ill people has become an increasing source of concern. Considerable anxiety and poor publicity has been generated about community care which is seen as not only neglecting this group of people, but effectively adding to their numbers through ill-considered and poorly coordinated discharge policies. The discussion of this issue in Chapter 1 served to clarify some of the misunderstanding surrounding this area and it will not be restated here. Rather this section will concentrate on what practically can be achieved in providing a more effective service to this group.

When reviewing services which have attempted to meet the mental health needs of homeless mentally ill people three common themes emerge: the poor provision of suitable accommodation, the multiple nature of the problems presented and the difficulties of maintaining contact in a coordinated manner. It is clear that many programmes which provide support for homeless mentally ill people fall down because of lack of residential backup (Baxter and Hopper, 1984). Leach (1979) describes some of the ways in which homeless people can be introduced into a range of accommodation. Often this accommodation is established by voluntary organisations and is open to a range of homeless people. The first step in ensuring appropriate psychiatric care comes from forging effective links with such settings and local health services. Homeless mentally ill people have a wide range of health problems; chronic mental illnes is prominent but so are a range of physical problems, particularly dermatological and respiratory ones (Timms and Fry, 1989). Of the psychiatric problems the major problem is that of schizophreina and not of alcohol abuse, although homeless individuals with alcohol-related problems may present most frequently to the services.

The multi-faceted nature of the problems presented has implications for the type of health care provided, suggesting that a comprehensive approach is necessary involving professionals outside of the traditional multi-disciplinary mental health team. Hamid and McCarthy (1989), in a study of the service provided by a Community Psychiatric Nursing Service to homeless mentally ill people, revealed a high drop-out rate amongst this group when compared to a home-based control. They suggest the high drop-out was in part due to a lack of skills within a uni-disciplinary team. The high drop-out rate also highlights the problem of coordinating services for the homeless mentally ill. A number of possible solutions can be considered. These include the establishment of a register, which would need adequate back up, perhaps by an assertive case management system such as is described in Chapter 6. It could be also addressed through the creation of a specialist multi-disciplinary team, such as that referred to by Timms and Fry (1989) which would need to be based in and around the facilities most used by homeless people and not in a traditional out-patient setting.

# THE ORGANISATION OF RESIDENTIAL SERVICES

The need for coordination of residential services is highlighted by the problems experienced by homeless mentally ill people. An effective rehabilitation service should be clear about its priorities. Given the wide range of individuals and agencies involved in the provision of supported housing there is a need for a forum where these priorities can be agreed and responses coordinated. Through proper coordination real opportunities can develop for the sharing of relevant skills and the maximisation of financial and other development resources. Coordinated services should be able to respond more effectively to changes in residents' needs than it is possible for isolated agencies or individuals to do. Coordination also builds links between agencies and broadens understanding of the difficulties faced by each agency which in turn leads to a fuller understanding of the difficulties faced by clients.

There are a number of mechanisms by which this coordination may be achieved. It may develop out of good practice being formalised by the creation of one or two posts to facilitate coordination as is the case in the service described by Howatt *et al.* (1988). Alternatively a consortium may be established specifically to develop and promote residential services. A number of such consortia exist, usually built around the provision of residential services and with a strong interest in obtaining maximum financial benefits under the Social Security legislation. Such consortia may cover all the services in a particular authority or district, be restricted to the needs of particular care groups or be established for one residential scheme only. A fuller discussion of some of the options available and the issues raised is provided by Bayliss (1987). With the publication of the White Paper, *Caring for People* (DHSS, 1989), the leading role of the local authority is made explicit. It remains to be seen how effective local authorities will be in the coordination of residential services and in promoting and maintaining innovation. Whatever the outcome, and it will be some years before the full effects are apparent, there will be considerable local variation and this may provide opportunities for staff to take a role in the development of coordinated services. This can be achieved through joint collaboration on specific projects or by the development of mechanisms for the coordination of individual care. Examples of the former include the development of small core and cluster housing schemes where a range of agencies contribute to both the provision and support of residencies. McAusland (1985) discusses the issues involved in establishing such settings for mentally ill people. A number of systems for the coordination of the individual care are described in this chapter and in the discussion of case management in Chapter 6.

## SUPPORTING STAFF IN RESIDENTIAL UNITS

At several points in this chapter the central role of direct care staff in ensuring the success of services has been emphasised. In this final section the support of direct care staff will be considered from two perspectives. First, the management and organisation of the duties and responsibilities of direct care staff and secondly, the role of external staff in providing support. Although the question of staff support is addressed seperately it should not be considered in isolation from staff training, the monitoring of services and the management arrangements for services.

Essential for the development of any effective support system is an understanding of the problems faced by staff in residential or other care settings. Many of the problems faced by staff have already been described in Chapter 4. These problems can manifest themselves as staff burn out which is characterised by apathy about the work task, resentment towards service users, high rates of absenteeism and high rates of staff turnover. The PSSRU research into community care, previously referred to (p. 88), considered the development of effective means to counteract the effects of staff burn out as essential to long-term success of community care. The following areas were identified as presenting particular problems to staff in residential settings: the lack of or the slow pace of client change, a lack of technical skills to cope with challenging behaviours, the increased demands of shift patterns, the blurring of roles to the point at which staff felt themselves to be 'jacks of all trades and masters of none' and increased client dependence. These problems can be exacerbated by the sense of isolation experienced by many direct care workers in small separate community-based units. In some of the services described the kind of defensive structures described by Menzies (1960) had come into operation.

For direct care staff the following activities can help to counteract burn out and support staff. Staff should participate in the development of a setting's philosophy and operational policies. Within the limits set by such factors as confidentiality and workload demands, as many staff as possible should be involved in the development of individual care programmes which will result in a clearer understanding of different staff members' contribution and also the setting's overall direction. Senior staff should be involved in direct care, as well as providing good and regular supervision. Senior staff also have a vital role in representing the interests of the staff to the outside world. In small community-based units flexibility with regard to shift patterns should be allowed, with as much responsibility for this as is possible being delegated to direct care staff. Regular and well-resourced training, both internal and external to the unit, can play a vital role in maintaining staff morale and combating the development of institutional practices. When there are particular challenges presented by a client in a residential setting the availability of adequate back-up staff to provide support is important as is cover for absences. In small units one staff member sick or on leave can expose other staff to considerable additional demands. There should also be proper mechanisms for linking in with other staff and agencies, through case reviews, educational visits, seminars and other means of informal contact.

The large mental hospital ensures a steady, if not always lively, stream of visitors to the ward and this ensures the ward does not become isolated, if only from the rest of the hospital. The same, however, cannot be said of small geographically separate units. Therefore, in addition to the activities referred to above, community-based support staff have a vital role in supporting direct care staff. There are a number of ways in which external staff can help. They can provide a fresh view of a familiar problem which staff close to the ground find difficult to resolve. They can provide direct clinical services to residents or take a role in facilitating the clients' use of other services. External staff can also be useful sources of information on developments in the locality. If sufficiently experienced, they may be able to offer supervision to direct care workers or establish a training programme around specific skills development. The facilitation of a staff support group is something which is best performed by an individual external to the care setting and if effective this can play a vital role in keeping the unit functioning effectively. On a more ambitious level an external staff member may support direct care staff through undertaking a major role in changing or developing care practices within a setting. In such circumstances the problem-solving model of organisational intervention is commonly adopted (Shepherd, 1984; Lavender, 1985). Essentially the model involves four stages: problem identification, development of strategies to overcome the problems, implementation of the strategies and finally evaluation of the strategies. Such work demands considerable skill and experience with support from several levels of the service system. Georgiades and Philmore (1975) offer some clues to effective intervention but also some words of caution, perhaps best expressed by the title of their paper 'The Myth of the Hero-innovator'. Sometimes helping care staff to cope with nothing very much changing is the most helpful thing to be done. As Shepherd (1988a) writes, when considering the negative symptoms of major mental illness '. . . [they] present problems that sometimes will not go away no matter how hard one tries. Living with this simple truth is, perhaps, the greatest challenge of all.'

*Chapter Six*

# DAY AND SUPPORT SERVICES

## INTRODUCTION

Day services were for many years at the forefront of community care. The establishment of the country's first day hospital in 1946 was accompanied by much enthusiasm about the reduction of stigma and institutionalisation. There was considerable hope that the services would also lead to substantial cost savings (Holloway, 1988b). From the immediate post-war years to the early 1970s, almost all developments in day services in the United Kingdom were led by the NHS and it was only with the establishment of local authority social services departments in 1971 that any major developments in day care took place outside the NHS. These early day services subscribed to a number of different models of the origins and treatment of mental illness. A number of different models of service organisation were developed. When local authorities became involved in the provision of day care it became necessary to have a clear policy for the organisation of day services. To this end a White Paper, *Better Services for the Mentally Ill* (DHSS, 1975), was produced by the Department of Health.

The 1975 White Paper drew a clear distinction between the treatment function and the long-term supportive function of day services. Day hospitals, run by health authorities, were to provide day treatment facilities primarily on a short-term basis. In contrast, day centres, run by local authorities, would provide long-term support services. However, within the document the potential for overlap in the provision of rehabilitation services was acknowledged. The paper also made specific recommendations about the numbers of places that should be provided based on the population of health and local authority areas.

Edwards and Carter (1979) conducted a national survey of day services and showed that provision in most areas fell short of the norms set out in the White Paper. They also reported that, despite staff awareness of the proposed difference in function of day hospitals and centres, the two services were often remarkably similar. Some differences in staffing were evident, with health authority units having a higher proportion of qualified staff. However, Edwards and Carter noted that the units had many more similarities than differences. Most had activities in common, with very similar percentages of time spent in social activities, on physical treatments, arts and crafts and work-related activities. The characteristics of the two client groups were also similar. To some extent this overlap of function could be accounted for by a lack of service provision, with few areas having both types of day unit. However, even where adequate provision of services existed, there was still considerable overlap of function. Edwards and Carter saw this as evidence of a lack of coordination between local social service departments and health authorities. Underlying this lack of coordination, were philosophical or ideological differences regarding the nature and treatment of mental illness. As a result a situation had arisen where the potential for the creative use of a diversity of models had been lost. Organisational failings and the pursuance of ideological causes, more appropriately dealt with through careful and thoughtful discussion than ill-considered experimentation, had resulted in inadequate service provision.

Ten years after the publication of the White Paper came official recognition of the problem when the Social Services Select Committee (1985) in its report on community care said of day care that there was 'confusion about what should be provided and by whom'. Despite this dawning awareness in official circles and a groundswell of opinion at the grassroots that all is not well, considerable problems remain (Vaughan, 1985). Many day services remain unclear about their function. There is serious concern about whether day services and similar services, such as community mental health centres, will ever give the priority to the long-term mentally ill that was originally intended (Sayce, 1987). The 1989 White Paper on community care, *Caring for*

*People,* had little to say about day care, concentrating on the provision of residential care and support services. However, with the closure of the large mental hospitals there will be an increasing demand for day services to play their part in the provision of community-based services. Bennett (Shepherd, 1984) has used the term 'up side down psychiatry' to stress the importance of day services over hospital beds. Perhaps we should adopt a similar 'up side down' notion of community care, stressing the importance of day and support services over residential care.

## THE NEED FOR DAY SERVICES

The needs of long-term service users have already been discussed in Chapter 1 when describing the results of the surveys of Wykes *et al.* (1982) and Brewin *et al.* (1988). In brief, these surveys showed a high proportion of unmet need amongst users of day services in a well-resourced inner-city area with 35 per cent of the individuals in the Wykes *et al.* and 44 per cent of the individuals in the Brewin *et al.* study having at least one unmet need. Unmet needs most commonly fell into the following areas; neurotic symptoms, positive psychotic symptoms, socially embarrassing behaviour, personal cleanliness, symptoms of physical disorder and use of public amenities. The most common area for over-provision of services concerned the over-prescription of psychotropic medication. Other studies have looked at clients' views of the services they received from day centres and hospitals. Davis (1985) summarised the outcome of a series of interviews with day service users. In these interviews users stressed the importance of the day centre in providing a place to go, allowing them to escape from the boredom of the house, the loneliness of walking the streets, or rather more positively the opportunity to mix with others and develop social relationships. Edwards and Carter (1979) asked day service clients to describe the ways in which they felt centres had been of help to them. The most frequent function of day units referred to by users was what Edwards and Carter described as the maintenance function of day care. As in the Davis' (1985) study, units were seen as providing a place to meet, a place where time could be occupied in some form of activity. Relatively little emphasis was placed on the treatment function of the units. In addition, less than 9 per cent of clients in the centres and 5 per cent of clients in the hospitals had any negative comments to make about the services they received. (These results should not be taken to imply an uncritical endorsement of the service but should be treated with caution as such surveys often report very high levels of satisfaction almost irrespective of the service provided (Baker and Intaglita, 1981).) When the effectiveness of the service was considered most clients saw the benefits of attendance as being solely to do with their functioning within the setting and commented very little on its impact outside the centres. Holloway (1989) provides further evidence that clients saw the benefits of day care attendance in social rather than therapeutic terms.

There is something of a paradox in the studies described above, Brewin *et al.* (1988) clearly identify unmet need in a number of therapeutic areas and yet there is apparently little concern amongst clients about the lack of services they receive in this area. This is a consistent finding across a number of studies (Holloway, 1989). Clearly differences in the methodology can account for some of the variation in these results. Nevertheless it is probable that both represent some version of the truth with regard to client need. Clients who may wish to deny that they are ill may not acknowledge that have needs for therapeutic services. They may be ignorant of some of the services that are available or they may be, perhaps appropriately, sceptical about their effectiveness. Professionals may, on the other hand, stress therapeutic activity at the expense of social support. The resolution of this paradox lies in the development of responsive assessment systems which actively involve the client and which are used not only to develop individual programmes of activity, but also to aid in the overall development of services.

## THE FUNCTIONS OF DAY SERVICES

The original distinction drawn in the 1975 White Paper between treatment and support remains a useful starting point for a consideration of the functions of day services for long-term mentally ill people. However, in order to fully understand the value of day services to this group, the distinction requires some elaboration. A list of the functions of day services is set out below:

1  As an alternative to hospital admission when an individual cannot be supported by out-patient services.
2  As a transitional phase between in-patient care and community residence
3  As a venue for a period of intensive treatment or rehabilitation for limited periods.
4  As a source of long-term support and rehabilitation.

The first three functions can be seen as treatment functions and were those that the White Paper saw as being provided by day hospitals. The fourth function, that of long-term support, would be provided by day centres. However, it is neither practical or desirable at the present time to equate function with setting; rather it is important to be clear about the distinction between these functions when developing a service. As will be seen later, when research on long-term day services is discussed, lack of clarity in this area has been to the considerable disadvantage of mentally ill people.

## TREATMENT APPROACHES TO DAY SERVICES

A number of authors have recently reviewed treatment approaches to day services, concentrating on acutely ill individuals (e.g. Herz, 1982; Rosie, 1987). The position with regard to the efficacy of such services is summarised by Rosie who writes:

The validity of the day hospital as an economical, effective treatment alternative for a substantial number of acutely ill patients is firmly established by well-designed, large scale, controlled and replicated studies. Further research on the general validity of day hospitals would be superfluous.

However, Rosie suggests that an increase in our understanding of who can be best helped in what way by these intensive treatment programmes is required.

The relative value of day services to a range of acutely ill people will not be discussed in this chapter; rather the concern will be with day treatment services for long-term mentally ill people. This is of particular importance when the potentially harmful effects of hospitalisation for long-term mentally ill people are considered (see Chapter 5). Day treatment can be effective for long-term mentally ill people. Fallon and Talbot (1982) demonstrated in their study of day treatment that, with carefully planned goal-orientated individual programmes, day patients with schizophrenia did better than other less disabled groups of patients. A number of studies have explored the use of day hospitals as an alternative to in-patient care. All have demonstrated in varying degrees the benefits of day hospitalisation over standard in-patient care (for example, Herz *et al.*, 1977; Gudeman *et al.*, 1985). In Gudeman *et al.* (1985) study all people requiring more intensive support than could be provided in the community were first assessed in a day hospital. This unit was the focus for all intensive treatment programmes. It was backed up by a 27-bedded intensive care unit and an 'Inn' which provides accommodation for those people who cannot support themselves with appropriate help in the community. The 'Inn' provides a means by which the hospitalisation of long-term mentally ill people could be avoided. (Such an approach bears some similarity to that of Stein and Test (1980) where hospitalisation was avoided by the provision of a higher level of support in people's homes or by the provision of temporary accommodation in community settings.) Wherever individuals were placed, continuity of care was provided by the day hospital team responsible for that individual. By working in this way Gudeman *et al.* were able to report a reduction in the number of people requiring in-patient care from 81 per cent to 56 per cent, as well a reduction in the total amount of time spent in hospital.

Studies such as those described above, give considerable support to the view that day treatment services have a significant role in the provision of community services. They reduce the need for periods of hospitalisation but do not eliminate the need for such services. Where hospitalisation is necessary they can contribute to a significant reduction in length of stay. These results can be achieved for chronically ill people with an acute exacerbation of their symptoms as well as with acutely ill people. However, rehabilitation is much more than the acute treatment of symptoms and it needs a long-term perspective. To be content with the day treatment centre replacing the in-patient unit would be to run the risk of simply recreating a new institution with all the potential failings of the old one. Indeed, there is some evidence that the long-term and ill-considered provision of the kind of services often seen in day hospitals can have negative effects for long-term mentally ill people, increasing their non-attendance at the settings (Bender and Pilling, 1985) and having negative therapeutic effects where they do stay (Linn *et al.*, 1979). This issue will be taken up in more detail in the discussion that follows.

## *Rehabilitation day services*

This section will concentrate on two areas of day services; those social and rehabilitative services built around various types of day centre and those built around some kind of work-related activity. Inevitably there is some overlap between these functions but it is important to see the distinction between them. It is clear from the discussion of users' views above that there are certain features of day care, such as the social contact it promotes, which are valued. Such activities meet needs that are common to all people. Yet these are activities which highly trained staff, often as a result of their training, place little value on; hence the need to be clear about the functions of day service and the relative importance of the various functions.

## *Centre based services*

Traditionally most day services have been provided within day units, but as the discussion above has highlighted these centres often suffer from lack of clarity about their role. In addition to the confusion between treatment and support there is often uncertainty about the kind of support and rehabilitation it is appropriate to provide. Some possible functions are set out below:

1 The provision of a venue(s) for the development of social relationships.
2 The provision of personal and social support to clients and their carers.
3 The provision of training in a range of community, personal and daily living skills.
4 The provision of a venue for a range of leisure activities.

5 The promotion of integration into and use of a range of community resources.

6 The provision of work-related activity.

These functions have traditionally been based in a day centre or day hospital which has catered for mentally disabled people. Indeed some centres carry out most, if not all, of these functions successfully. However, when these various functions are carefully considered and compared with much existing practice it becomes increasingly difficult to avoid the conclusion that attempts to provide for all these activities on one site are fraught with difficulty, both for service users and providers. (When considering developments in day care it is helpful to remember that Stein and Test (1980) saw good community care as providing what the person needs, when he needs it and where it will do most good.) What now follows is a description of a range of services currently available as models on which future developments may be based. Where available the evidence for their effectiveness is given.

## The 'drop-in'

'Drop-ins' are the wild flowers of mental health care, they can pop up anywhere, sometimes in the most unexpected places. Their popularity indicates that they fulfil a real need, essentially for a place to meet with others over a cup of tea, a cigarette and a biscuit. For socially isolated people they can be life savers. Their variety is infinite; they can be large, complex self-supporting organisations or they can be once-a-week meetings with no more facilities than a room, a kettle and a few pounds to cover the cost of tea and biscuits. Like wild flowers their life can be short, especially if they are not well established. Often they respond poorly to cultivation (that is input from the statutory services), whose formalised methods can stifle their growth. They play a particularly important role for those people who find a high degree of social contact threatening or overstimulating, providing what Mitchell and Birley (1983) have referred to as 'company without intimacy'. The majority of such services are provided by the voluntary sector and this is likely to remain the case. The role of the statutory sector should be restricted largely to that of funding.

However, as the importance of less structured services for mentally ill people begins to be recognised by the statutory services, developments have occurred. This has usually happened in one of two ways. First, the statutory service has a direct relationship as a funder with the individuals using that service rather than through the intermediary of a voluntary organisation. Secondly, and increasingly popular, is one aspect of the service provided by a day centre is established as a drop-in. An example of the former is the Tontine Road Mental Health Centre in Derbyshire (Milroy, 1985), where the centre is given over to a wide range of activities and the staff function to facilitate the use of the centre by various user groups who have the major say in the direction of the centre. The activities are more or less formalised in content and structure and can take place in the centre; alternatively the centre is used as a base for the coordination of activities external to it. Many day centres now open their doors on a weekly basis to provide a drop-in or turn over the facilities of the centre to a local voluntary group for such purposes. Such arrangements have the considerable advantage of allowing the service to remain in touch with individuals with whom they would otherwise have little or no contact. In addition to tea and biscuits and a chat, a number of services have grown up which provide for specific functions. Typically, these can involve the provision of a meal on a weekly or daily basis, at a cheap rate. Other services have included the sale of food at a wholesale price, the provision of advice about benefits or the organisation of a second-hand clothes shop.

## The clubhouse model

The strength of the drop-in lies in its flexibility but as has been pointed out above, there is often a price to be paid, that of an uncertain future. This is a real concern for people with long term mental illness who need continuity of service and have some difficulty in establishing a place in any social setting. One model, which combines security with the degree of flexibility and client involvement characteristic of the better drop-ins, is the Clubhouse pioneered by John Beard and others at Fountain

House in the United States (Beard *et al.*, 1982). As the name suggests individuals become members of the club and are then entitled to the benefits of membership and also have to take on the responsibilities of membership. Many of the activities in which members engage are concerned with the running and maintenance of the club. This is arranged around work groups concerned with providing the domestic services to the club, the catering, the club's clerical services, the club's social activities and so on. There is ample opportunity within this range of activity for individuals with different abilities and needs to find a niche where they can make their distinct contribution to the organisation. Clubhouses are available to members 7 days a week, 52 weeks a year with a strong emphasis on activities in the evening, at weekends and during holidays.

The clubhouse also promotes the return to employment of its members through the provision of temporary employment placements (TEPs). In a TEP it is possible for an individual to have the experience of a six-month placement in ordinary employment which is paid at the full rate. Although encouraged to take the opportunity to return to employment, there is no requirement on any individual to do so. Membership is for life and individuals are able to make what use of the centre they wish, retaining links through social events and other meetings long after they may have left any formal programme at the centre. The clubhouse also places a strong emphasis on maintaining contact with members, in particular with those who drop out, through an assertive outreach programme which puts the initial responsibility on members to follow up absent colleagues. The success of the clubhouse model can be measured by the fact that since the late 1950s, when the first club was established, over 170 similar clubs have been created in the United States.

## The day centre

Many drop-ins and clubhouses share one thing in common, they are clear about their purpose. This is in marked contrast to many day centres. Most offer a range of services on one site which is more often indicative of confusion over purpose and function than it is of a wide range of choice available to service users. Such confusion often arises at the planning stage and is the result of too much being expected of too little, with the consequence that a multitude of potentially contradictory goals are identified for the centre. Where this is the case staff are often left to make choices in the absensce of clear priorities or guiding principles. In such circumstances choices, not suprisingly, often reflect staff rather than client need. However the inadequacy of provision and uncertainty of purpose at all levels of the service system have resulted in the problems, when combined with a high demand for services, being ignored or misunderstood. For example, Bender and Pilling (1985) studied a large multi-purpose mental health day centre. The centre provided a wide range of psychological treatments, work-related activity and social support. They looked, in particular, at the drop-out rate from this setting and found that it was accounted for almost entirely by the group for which the centre was largely intended, that is, long-term mentally ill people. In this centre, where staff prioritised the verbal therapies, long-term mentally ill people felt over-stimulated and so excluded themselves. Linn *et al.* (1979), in a much larger study of day care for people with schizophrenia, report similar results. On examining a number of outcome variables in a range of day centres, they showed poor outcome to be associated with a higher level of professional staff, a high rate of client turnover, and an emphasis on verbal therapies. In contrast, occupational therapy and a 'sustained non-threatening environment' were associated with good outcome.

Two solutions are typically adopted by day centres when seeking a way out of these problems; both of them concerned to open up the system to external influence. The first approach acknowledges the limits imposed by the demands of differing functions and resource constraints. Centres develop clear priorities and set limited goals. Inevitably this means restricting the access to the centre to certain client groups. Such an approach has been developed by the London Borough of Kensington and Chelsea (Blake *et al.*, 1984). The day centres in the borough, all of which are described as therapeutic communities, serve different client groups, which can be crudely characterised in terms of their ability or aptitude to use structured group activities. This may range from required attendance at a daily psychotherapy group in one setting, to dropping in on the daily group when the mood takes one in another. The emphasis on verbal or non-verbal methods of working varies with the interest and aptitudes of the clients. In such a service it is possible to retain clarity about goals, guided by clear principles that underlie the service. However, such an approach makes large demands on resources and requires a high level of staff skill. Given the dearth of services referred to previously, if is unlikely to be adopted on a widespread basis. Such an arrangement also runs the risk of excluding the most diasabled. It does, however, highlight the value of clarity about goals and there are elements of the model which can be adopted to other day services. For example, within a day centre it is possible to design programmes for different client groups who attend for activities at different times in .the week. Such an approach may require a much more flexible use of staff than has been the case in the past. However, increased flexibility brings increased strain and if programmes along these lines are to be developed a considerable input into staff support is required.

The second option concentrates on opening up the centre by making it a base for the coordination and enabling of activity rather than the only place where activity occurs. This is achieved both by opening the centre to the local community and by establishing clients in a range of locally-based services. In such a centre clients may attend the centre for only a limited number of sessions per week, if at all; many of the activities associated with the centre taking place outside of the building in community halls, local education departments, parks and cafes. The Erconwald Centre (Embelton, 1985) is one example of such a service. The centre, based in West London, offers a range of activities to clients. Some, such as group activities take place in the centre. Other activities, such as a weekly Food Co-op, are run jointly with the local tenants association. Other activities take place outside of the centre and include attendance at local education classes, training in daily living skills (more effective if it is done in people's own homes) or drop-ins in a range of more accessible venues. The centre also opens its doors to the local community, providing space for the tenants association and a parents and children's drop-in. Such an approach facilitates integration but is not without difficulties which are well described by Embleton.

The more specialised one service becomes, the more dispersed another, the greater is the need for coordination. Much of the discussion of community care has centred on the provision of accommodation and the development of individual coordination systems, relatively little attention being devoted to day services. Effective day services must be coordinated to ensure priorities are properly addressed and this requires clear policies across the health, local authority and voluntary agencies. This should help to prevent the duplication of function which is inexcusable when resources are scarce. Such coordination does not necessitate the central management of resources but rather a commitment to joint working. For example, through the creation of a joint referral system or method of review.

## Work-related services

The importance of work-related activity in rehabilitation services has waxed and waned over the years. The early Victorian mental hospitals had their own farms and were virtually self-supporting communities with their own dressmakers, breweries and shoemakers. However, during the first half of this century, as the hospitals became overcrowded and demoralised institutions, work-related activity fell away only to be revived after the Second World War. Work-related activity was to play a crucial part in the early move towards community care (Early and Magnus, 1968). However, the 1960s and 1970s again saw a decline in work-related activity. It was not only neglected, but was often seen as indicative of the worst kind of institutional practice. More recently there has been a resurgence of interest in work-related services (Pilling, 1988b).

When considering the role of work-related activity in community care it is helpful to understand the importance of work in society. Freud (1930) wrote that no other activity 'attaches the individual so firmly to reality as laying emphasis on work' and its psychological significance has long been realised. One of the clearest conceptualisations of the psychological importance of work is provided by Jahoda (1981). At this point it is helpful to distinguish between work and employment. Work is defined as purposeful activity requiring judgement and discretion which has social significance and is subject to external constraints. Employment is defined as the exchange relationship which exists between employer and employee as a result of work performed. Jahoda argues that work (or more specifically employment) is unique in the psychological functions that it performs. By using her distinction between the latent and manifest functions of employment we can gain some understanding of the psychological importance of work and also some guidance on the principles that should underlie any work-related rehabilitation service. The manifest functions of employment are the terms and conditions of employment. The latent functions of employment (and here the meaning is synomonous with work) are as follows: the imposition of a time structure, the enforcement of activity, the development of goals which transcend one's own, the development of social relationships outside the primary group and the definition of personal status.

It is readily obvious to anyone familiar with the difficulties faced by people with long-term mental illness that the latent functions of work address problems which are at the centre of many mentally ill people's daily struggle; loss of status, social isolation and difficulty in structuring time. Pilling (1988b) has reviewed the evidence for the effectiveness of work-related activity in rehabilitation which demonstrates not only the potential efficacy of work-related activity in community-based services but also gives guidance on the most appropriate methods for service delivery. Work-related activity has value both in aiding the successful rehabilitation and resettlement of people and providing a positive means of occupying individuals who will continue to require long-term support. However, despite the considerable evidence in favour of work-related activity there remains, at best, an ambivalence, amongst most mental health professionals towards it. Shepherd (1989a) considers some of the reasons behind this ambivalance including staff anxieties about their own work, the supposed contradiction in helping 'sick' people to work and the uneasiness felt by many health authorities in providing work opportunities. He does however conclude that 'for many chronic psychotic patients work . . . may be the most effective treatment we have'.

In what follows some guidelines on the establishment of community-based work-related activity are provided and where appropriate they are accompanied by examples drawn from existing schemes. At the present time much of the work-related activity of the mental health services still takes place in large hospitals with units for 50 or more people. This is often the case even when there has been significant development of community-based residential services. Although many of these hospital-based workshops continue to provide a valuable service, it is clear that provision of residential places is given much greater priority and there is a serious threat to the long term survival of such units if they do not develop a community base. Units of 30 people or less, sited near to existing manufacturing or service industries are ideal. Small disused factories or more modern small industrial units are equally serviceable. Adequate funding of services is vital. They cannot be expected to make a profit and the statutory authorities have a clear responsibility for such funding. With some work schemes, particularly those involved in the preparation of individuals for some form of employment, opportunities exist for sources of funding beyond the usual statutory services, such as the Manpower Services Commission (MSC).

A number of services, in particular the government sponsored Employment Rehabilitation Centres or the 'Remploy' sheltered factories provide for a range of disabled groups and there is a trend in some quarters to develop work schemes along similar lines. This trend should be viewed with some caution. There is good reason to support the placement of mentally ill people who are preparing for a return to open employment in preparation units with non-disabled people. However, mentally ill people are likely to require a longer period of preparation in such settings than other individuals (Cornes et al., 1982). A number of schemes can provide supported work opportunities. For example, Sheltered Placement Schemes, which are sponsored by the MSC, provide real work opportunities in which a disabled individual is placed in a regular job, supported by experienced staff and paid the full rate. The employer is reimbursed for that percentage below which the individual performs when compared to a non-disabled person in the same post. Another scheme is the Temporary Employment Placement previously mentioned in the discussion of Fountain House (Beard et al., 1982). Where individuals are too disabled or disinclined for other reasons to seek supported or open employment then it is preferable that single disability work settings are created. If not, there is a real risk that the mixing of disabilities will serve only to reinforce stigma.

111

A number of projects have developed techniques for placing and mantaining people in open employment. Jacobs *et al.* (1984) describe a 'Job Club' which significantly improved both the job finding ability of long-term mentally ill people and also, through the provision of continuing support, enabled them to stay in employment. The Job Club was essentially a skills training programme which focused on the skills necessary to find employment. It also made extensive use of peer support in maintaining people in employment. This is of particular value because, as Floyd (1984) has shown, many more long-term mentally ill people give up their jobs as a result of stresses encountered than are ever dismissed.

Payment remains a major problem in most settings. Few schemes pay anything approaching an ordinary wage, such as provided by an SPS or TEP. The position is considerably complicated by the restrictions placed on people's earnings by the rules governing social security payments. These benefit rules have recently been relaxed after having been unchanged for over fifteen years. The situation remains unsatisfactory and requires both additional resources and further relaxation in the legislation before an equitable situation is achieved.

Perhaps one of the biggest tasks facing both hospital and community-based work projects concerns the nature of work undertaken. Economic circumstances are forcing work units to move away from the declining market of light industrial work and sub-contract packing which has been their basic activity for the past 30 years. Many of the more successful community-based projects have focused on service activities. For example, the Many Hands project run by Kensington and Chelsea Mind in London trains individuals in painting and decorating skills. Many Hands continues to act as an 'agent' finding individuals work after they have completed their training. Other schemes provide furniture or toy repair services or run small cafes or sandwich services (see Pilling, 1988b for further detail). Whatever activity is chosen it needs to provide opportunities for the involvement of the most and the least disabled client. This means that it will need to combine a demand for skilled activity with the opportunity to perform simple routines requiring little training or concentration, but which nevertheless have an identified end product. It may be possible to provide for all these activities on one site in a large multi-purpose work unit or, for example, through the development of a project for selling wholefood which demands a range of skills from marketing to the routine packaging of beans.

The final issue to be considered is the staffing of the unit. It is clear that a different attitude is required from staff than is required in most treatment settings. In certain units an entrepreneurial spirit is also needed if the project is to be successful. Such skills are not often found in the mental health professions and this, combined with the tendency of some staff to turn even the most mundane activity in to some kind of 'therapy', means that the bulk of staff for these units must be drawn from outside the statutory services. However, Harding *et al.* (1987) provide a disturbing account of the difficulties that arise when clear lines are drawn between those clinical staff involved in the provision of 'therapeutic' services and those involved in the provision of work-related rehabilitation services. In their study of services in New Haven, Connecticut, they demonstrate that the mutual ignorance of clinicians and vocational rehabilitation workers has detrimental effects on clients. A first step in overcoming these familiar difficulties is the acceptance of the valuable function of work in rehabilitation and beyond that a clear commitment to develop systems that allow for regular exchange of skills and knowledge between the different staff groups. Effective input into joint assessment and programme planning systems can help. In the United Kingdom where many work units are still in hospital settings, the opportunities for cooperation are much increased and it will be important in community-based settings that the role of mental health professionals in the support of staff and clients in work rehabilitation units is maintained.

## COMMUNITY SUPPORT SERVICES

The emphasis so far in this and the previous chapter has been on services provided in or by settings, for example services based on a day centre or provide by a group home. This is clearly a very important part of community care. However, they are elements of the service in which the majority of long-term mentally ill people spend relatively little time and in which a minority spend no time at all. A number of services which can provide intensive rehabilitation services to individuals in community settings have already been described (for example, Stein and Test, 1980; Hoult and Reynoulds, 1984). There is a need to develop services of a different nature for many other people, particularly with the increasing dispersal of services for long-term mentally ill people throughout the community. This need has long been recognised and has been influential in the development of the role of the Community Psychiatric Nurse (CPN) in this country and the Community Mental Health Centre (CMHC) in the United States.

The recognition of this need and the provision of resources has not been matched by the delivery of services. CMHCs, which are increasingly a part of the services in this country, have been characterised by a drift away from the care of the more severely mentally disabled to the 'worried well'. This process has been well documented in the United States (Holloway, 1988b), and there is some evidence to support the view that a similar process is happening in the United Kingdom (Sayce, 1987). This process is in marked contrast to what has happened in the large mental hospitals where there has been an increase in the number of severely disabled people (Ford *et al.*, 1987). With regard to the CPN, there is evidence that the location of CPNs in primary care settings has resulted in their isolation from the multi-disciplinary perspective necessary for effective rehabilitation. This has had a negative impact on the care of long-term mentally ill people (Wooff and Goldberg, 1988).

Many community-based services lack effective systems for the identification and monitoring of long-term mentally ill people. As a result many slip through the net and in the absence of clearly stated priorities are not followed up. In the United States this has led to the development of a range of community support systems and case management systems of which Phipps and Liberman (1988) provide a useful overview. Case management systems are becoming of increasing importance and will be discussed in some detail below after a review of existing support systems in the United Kingdom.

The development of community support systems in the United Kingdom has been uneven, with some individuals or districts developing local initiatives, often built on good multi-disciplinary care. The same is true of the United States where development has been patchy. Until the recent White Paper (DHSS, 1989) there has been little in the way of central directives. As a consequence the most developed system is that of the 'key worker' in which an identified member of staff is responsible for the coordination of an agreed programme plan. In key worker systems the emphasis is on the coordination of care rather than its delivery and in many systems the key worker may have little involvement in the assessment of the client's need. Such systems have often evolved most effectively in hospital environments where they are compatible with existing multi-disciplinary models of working. However, it is doubtful whether such models are sufficiently well developed to address the needs of those individuals served by a much more dispersed community system.

The Department of Health has sponsored a number of pilot projects of computerised registers for long-term mentally ill people in the community. One such system is that described by Whitehead (1987) which was based on a multi-disciplinary community team serving a distinct catchment area in Salford. The system was based on a multi-disciplinary assessment completed by appropriate members of the team. A multi-disciplinary review was held and a goal-orientated programme plan developed with a specific key worker being given responsibility for the coordination and implementation of the programme. The system proved effective at developing individual care plans and seems to provide useful guidance on how existing practices can be improved. However, it also raised a number of important questions. The work involved was much more time consuming and demanding than had been envisaged, with only half of the intended reviews completed in the first year of the project. Perhaps more importantly the project uncovered a good deal of unmet need for which there was often no available provision. This proved to be a dispiriting experience for both staff and clients and caused them to question the value of such an exercise in the face of limited resources. Such a finding also raises an important question about the value of registers in general, as they are sometimes seen as a solution to keeping in contact with long-term mentally ill people in the community. It is clear from the Salford study that registers could become an excuse for inaction if the teams responsible for maintaining the register are not sufficiently resourced to allow for effective care planning. Effectively resourced registers can be an invaluable tool in developing understanding of patterns of local need (Walsh,

1985). They can also be adapted, as demonstrated by Martindale (1987) (see Chapter 3) in another Department of Health sponsored project, to provide information systems not only for professional staff but also for clients and their informal supporters.

## Case management systems

Both the systems described above could be said to be a form of case management. Case management systems (CMS) for long-term mentally ill people have largely been developed in the United States, although there have been a number of pilot schemes developed for disabled groups in this country, for example, the scheme developed for frail elderly people by Kent Social Services (Challis and Davis, 1986). Case management does not refer to any one method of care coordination but a wide range of models sharing the common feature of an identified individual (or less frequently a team of individuals) responsible for the care of an individual client. Typically in well developed case management system the responsibilities of case managers include:

1 Identification of clients who need case management.
2 Working with the client on the assessment of need.
3 Development of an appropriate programme plan which includes consideration of informed choice by the client.
4 Assisting the client to link into appropriate services
5 Monitoring provision of the identified services.
6 Evaluating client progress.

The above functions are usually performed in the context of a long-term supportive relationship which is flexible in nature. The adoption of a case management system offers mental health services a number of options, ranging from a radical restructuring of the whole organisation to a gentle refurbishment of the existing model, building on and enhancing its existing strengths and virtues. In the discussion that follows some of the relevant dimensions of case management systems will be set out, highlighting the choices that are available.

The role of the case manager

The functions outlined above represent the minimum that is

usually accepted to be a full case management system. If these functions are to be assigned to one individual, it represents a significant shift away from the multi-disciplinary based system common to most community-based teams in this country where the above functions are dispersed amongst team members. The advantages of adopting such a system in this country are at present unknown, although they are currently the subject of an extensive research progranmme in several health districts (Clifford and Craig, 1989). At the moment we can only look to reports on CMSs from the United States. Bond *et al.* (1988), in a follow-up of a CMS, describe how the functioning of the system was improved when case managers from a range of professional backgrounds ceased to work independently but instead began to work cooperatively as teams. The task also generally seemed easier where there were strong linkages between the CMS and other aspects of the mental health service, for example sharing the same office building. Some CMS are established as team based operations from the beginning e.g. Borland *et al.* (1989).

In the standard multi-disciplinary team there is an implicit acceptance of the therapeutic role of all members of the team. For example, in the Salford Community Project referred to above all members of the team could potentially take on therapeutic tasks. With the CMS that have developed in the United States the question of whether or not case managers take on therapeutic roles with clients is at the centre of the debate on the future of CMS. The choice is between a brokerage model of CMS which sees the case manager as a procurer of services and one of which sees the case manager as a therapist who also takes on responsibility for the coordination of care. Much of the debate about which of the two models to choose stems from concern about the development of advocacy roles for the case manager and the difficulty inherent in being both a provider and procurer of services. Even where there has been a clear decision about the choice of model a good deal of overlap occurs in practice. The very considerable strains on individual staff imposed by the many tasks demanded by case management also need to be borne in mind when systems are being established.

Who should be case managers

The key factor in determining who should be case managers is the management arrangements for the CMS. Existing agencies such as health or social services could individually or jointly take on responsibility for the system or a new agency could be created specifically to provide case management services. Whatever system is chosen it will need considerable resources if it is to be effective and this strongly argues against any form of duplication. In the United States many independent agencies have been established to provide case management services (for example, Harris and Bergman, 1988) but the provision of accessible locally-based health and social services is much more limited in the United States than it is in this country. If there is a general rule about which agency should have case management responsibility then it should be the one which has the best developed service and therefore requires the least change to ensure effective implementation. In many areas this means that the role may naturally fall to the CPN or to members of a well established community rehabilitation team. The White Paper, in stressing the role of case management, specifies a list of functions similar to those listed above and acknowledges the importance of flexibility in allocating case management roles, there being no requirement that it should be restricted to local authority staff. Whoever takes on the role they will need to be as concerned with individuals' social needs as with their therapeutic needs. The benefit office needs to be as familiar a venue as the out-patient suite.

A considerable debate has also developed in the United States concerning the training and qualifications of case managers. Lamb (1980) has argued for the role to be encompassed within that of the clinical members of the multi-disciplinary team, others for the creation of a new profession of case manager (Kanter, 1989) and others have chosen to develop a generic non-professional case management role (Sherman, 1988). Given the very different circumstances existing in the two countries it is unclear precisely what can be learned from the United States. It is, however, clear that the functions of case management described above do need to be carried out and the very wide nature of the resources needed by long-term mentally ill people should be borne in mind. These include not only health services but housing, income support, work and vocational activity, friendship and leisure activity. Such a range of activity clearly demands the input of more than one individual or agency and of course makes a considerable demand on resources. The creation of case management systems alone will do little to solve these problems.

## Conclusion

Given the very considerable problems in implementation encountered by many CMS it seems probable that extending the role of existing clinical staff offers the most promising way forward. This probably is best done in the context of a multi-disciplinary team as it provides a range of effective support and alternative perspectives that are needed to ensure effective rehabilitation work (Wooff and Goldberg, 1988). What is required is not a new system or profession but the adequate resourcing of the existing system with a clarification of service priorities and the development of effective monitoring arrangements. The creation of a team within the local community mental health services seems to be the way forward. Clear links with mental health services are vital. This can be most easily achieved through the appointment of staff with responsibilities to both CMS and other mental health services. Where this does not happen then great care will be needed to ensure that those served by CMS do not become marginalised and therefore not integrated into existing mental health services.

## Chapter Seven

# FAMILIES AND OTHER CARERS

### INTRODUCTION

Families have always had the central role in the care of the mentally ill. The advent of community care has not significantly changed the burden for the majority of families whose relatives have always spent most of their time outside of the large mental hospitals. However, the position of an important minority, those whose relatives were or are currently long-term residents of the large mental hospitals, has been the focus of considerable public attention. There is considerable concern about the potential burden that community care will place on them. This concern has often been ignored and has led to a politicisation of the role of families in community care movement. This has resulted in a polarisation of viewpoints. Families and their allies (including significant professional opinion) are often set against community care (which in these circumstances is synonymous with hospital closure) and against pressure groups which are seen as promoting community care (often including patient/user groups). It is one of the tragedies of community care that a potentially powerful ally, both in the United Kingdom and in the United States, has been pushed into opposition to community care. A major responsiblity for this lies with those professionals and planners who have advocated community care without consultation with families. Families have been crudely stigmatised, labelled as 'schizophrenogenic' and effectively disqualified from any constructive involvement in the debate. Significant advances in family treatment approaches to mental illness have been poorly presented to families (Strachan, 1986)

120

and have resulted in alienation and not support. As McCarthy (1988) states the lessons of these early mistakes are now being learned but much damage has been done and considerable effort will have to be made to recover the situation. (Throughout this chapter reference will be made to families but much of the material is applicable to any individual(s) who live with or support a mentally ill person in a non-professional relationship.)

## THE NATURE OF FAMILY BURDEN

The term 'family burden' was first used by Grad and Sainsbury (1968) and is taken by Platt (1985) to refer to 'the presence of problems, difficulties or adverse life events which affect the life (lives) of the psychiatric patients' significant others'. Platt provides a useful overview of the conceptualisation of family burden and the methods available for its measurement. Much of the research on family burden has concentrated on the subjective experience (guilt, anger, emotional involvement with the sufferer) of carers and how this impacts on the well-being of the mentally disabled person. However, as McCarthy (1988) points out, such an approach ignores the real objective stress that the carers of mentally disabled people face including loss of income, difficulties to be faced in coping with aggressive or anti-social behaviour, disruption to social life and problems with accommodation. These subjective and objective aspects of family burden have often been confused, and not just by researchers but by over-burdened relatives as well. As a result an inconsistent picture of the extent of family burden emerges in which it is difficult to tease out which problem is attributable to which cause. Such confusion can itself further exacerbate the burden. Lefley (1989) provides a useful review of family burden and points out that whilst some aspects of objective burden may be common to a number of chronic disabilities some are specific to mental illness. The most prominent of these is the fluctuating nature of the disorder. However, as Lefly puts it, 'Perhaps the most devastating stressor for families, however, is learning to cope with the patient's own anguish over an impoverished life.'

Whatever uncertainty exists about the nature and extent of family burden, considerable clarity emerges when families' views about service provision are examined. Services are seen as badly failing families. These failings often begin on initial contact with services, particularly around the first hospital admission. A pattern is then established of poor relations which can rapidly develop into chronic difficulties (McCarthy 1988; Griffin Francell *et al.*, 1988).

A good deal of relatives' dissatisfaction centres on the inadequate information they are given, particularly where treatment, diagnosis and the possible involvement of the family in treatment are concerned. Relatives find themselves excluded from many decisions about treatment, a process, often underpinned by simplistic theorising on the part of mental health professionals, which holds families responsible for their relatives' condition (Strachan, 1986). Unfortunately families often emerge from this confused, their tendency to blame themselves increased rather than reduced. The result is often a rejection by both parties of the help they have to offer to each other. This lack of mutual regard leads to a method of coping by families which centres on (often inadequate) crisis management. It ignores the more chronic problems, such as lack of motivation or social withdrawal, which contribute significantly to family burden and for which crisis management techniques are quite inappropriate. It is important to remember when relatives seem less than enthusiastic about the help that a rehabilitation team is offering that such people may have experienced years of rejection by professionals and consequently find it hard to match the team's enthusiasm. Such lack of enthusiasm can be mistaken for evidence of family psychopathology by those minded to do so.

In addition to a lack of information, carers report a number of other difficulties with services. A survey by Griffin Francell *et al.* (1988) lists a number which are commonly reported. They include a lack of services or support in crisis situations, with much buck-passing by professionals; poor provision of community resources (including day provision, residential services and adequate transport); absence of advice on the management of difficult behaviour; lack of continuity in care giving; non-involvement of relatives in treatment plans; and pressure to attend for family therapy sessions, the purpose of which is often unexplained to relatives. Lefley (1989) reports on a survey of mental health professionals with a chronically mentally ill relative. They describe many of the same problems as other carers with an increased potential for stigmatisation by their colleagues. Service failings can, therefore, be seen as adding significantly to the burden of families and other carers.

The consequences of this burden for carers are considerable. Creer *et al.* (1982) report that over 20 per cent of the relatives in the group they surveyed felt unable to leave their relatives alone even for a few hours. This meant having to cope with problems at least as challenging as those faced by staff in residential units, but without the support or breaks available to such staff. McCarthy *et al.* (1989) report that 93 per cent of a sample of relatives of long-term users of the day services of a London borough experienced some form of objective burden. It has been estimated (McCarthy, 1988) that approximately 30 per cent of relatives face serious psychiatric problems as a consequence of living with or supporting a mentally disabled relative. It appears that relatives find acute symptoms most distressing and immediately disruptive but the more chronic problems of social withdrawal and lack of motivation seem to impair the relationship between family and disabled person in the longer term (Birchwood and Smith, 1986). Where the onset of a chronic mental illness does not lead to the breakdown of a family or relationship, there is a progressive withdrawal from a range of social contacts on the part of carers with associated negative consequences for their psychological well-being.

## WORKING FAMILIES AND CARERS

Effective family work requires mutual trust and respect which must be based on an alliance between carer and professional staff. This alliance cannot be taken for granted and must be developed. It means that the differing needs of carers and their disabled relatives must be acknowledged. The underlying principles for the involvement of carers in the care of the long-term mentally ill are no different from those spelled out in previous chapters. The alliance must be built on a recognition of the legitimate interest that carers have in the welfare of their family member and the development of services for them. It must acknowledge and respond to the expressed needs of carers for information and education, advice on the management of difficult behaviour and for involvement with support groups. It can benefit from the acknowledgement of and support for carers' own organisations. At the individual level it means active involvement in the treatment programme for the majority of families and other carers but it also requires that services involve carers in planning and service development.

## Involvement in the planning process

There is widespread acknowledgement of the principle of involving service users in the planning of services but much less of the involvement of carers. Bringing families into this process can do much to overcome the suspicion that exists and help to develop a clearer understanding of service needs and direction. Existing organisations such as local branches of the National Schizophrenia Fellowship (NSF) offer an excellent base for such developments but individuals with commitment and ability can also be drawn on. The offer of such opportunities can go some way to help overcome the sense of resignation or alienation that is felt by many families.

## Education and information groups

The dearth of information made available to relatives has already been emphasised. One common response is to establish groups aimed specifically at increasing the information available to relatives. Smith and Birchwood (1987) describe a system where informatiom was made available to relatives through either four group sessions or written material sent by post. They were able to demonstrate that this produced an increase in relatives' knowledge of schizophrenia and a reduction in their reported level of stress but no change in patients' symptoms or level of disturbance. Although this is a quite positive result for a limited intervention, such results should be treated cautiously. Tarrier (1988), in reviewing the effectiveness of information groups, warns against simplistic models of information deficit amongst relatives. There is some evidence that they are less effective with relatives of individuals with chronic disorders and so may be better targeted at relatives of more acutely disturbed patients with recent onset of illness. It is probable that their main function with relatives of chronically disabled individuals will be in facilitating entry into the support or treatment programmes discussed below.

## Carer's support groups

Many areas of the country have support groups formed through organisations such as the NSF. These groups perform an important support function for relatives who may otherwise become isolated. Such groups are a valuable resource and should be supported and encouraged by the statutory services. They can provide a useful forum for educational inputs from mental health professionals. However, not all areas have a well developed NSF or similar organisation or, where one exists, some individuals may not wish to affiliate themselves. In such circumstances the statutory services should look to providing such a service.

Kuipers et al. (1989) describe one such service. The group was based in a well resourced day unit and relatives of long-term service users were offered the opportunity to attend. An intial assessment interview took place in the relatives' home, coupled with a single education session. This session was then followed by a monthly support group run along the lines of support groups in family intervention studies (see p. 127). The groups were educative and directive in nature avoiding analytic interpretation of past or present functioning. There was a strong emphasis on mutual support and problem solving, with ample opportunity for the sharing of feelings. The group met monthly (established by previous studies as the optimum time) for 18 months, then it came to a natural end. Kuipers et al. make a number of interesting observations about the group. First, they noted that being a mixed diagnostic group presented some difficulties for individuals with neurotic relatives who found it hard to comprehend many of the difficulties of the relatives of people with psychosis. In addition, it was apparent that individuals who had relatives with non-schizophrenic, but acute or fluctuating psychotic disorders did not receive the individual attention that they required. They emphasised the low-cost nature of the intervention and its feasibility in terms of the limited demands on time when compared to the family intervention models described below. McCarthy et al. (1989) evaluated the group against a control and reported significant gains in clients' domestic and self-help skills. The results are particularly interesting in that they took place in the context of a very well resourced day service which had already had systems for ensuring regular contact with patients' relatives. They point the way for future developments in a range of similar services.

## Specific family interventions

The origin of family interventions in long-term mental illness lies in the attempts to understand the cause of schizophrenia in terms of disturbance in family relationships. Over the past fifty years a number of hypotheses have been developed, for example, the notion of the 'schizophrenegenic mother' (Fromm-Reichmann, 1948) or the 'double bind' hypothesis of Bateson and his colleagues (Bateson *et al.*, 1956). However, despite many experimental studies, and widespread agreement on the presence of disordered communication in families where there is a family member with schizophrenia, no evidence of a causal link between patterns of family relationships and the development of schizophrenia has been found. (See Leff (1978) for a thorough review of these experimental studies.)

With the acceptance of the idea that family environments were not causally linked to schizophrenia, the focus shifted to the role of the family environment in the maintenance and development of symptoms. The most well developed work in this area is that of George Brown and his colleagues on Expressed Emotion (EE) (Brown *et al.*, 1962). This work has been used as the basis for a series of therapeutic interventions by Leff and his colleagues (Leff *et al.*, 1985). In common with many similar models of family intervention, Leff adopts a stress-diathesis model of schizophrenia.

Expressed Emotion is measured by a structured family interview (the Camberwell Family Interview) which is audiotaped and then rated on a number of key variables which can be used to derive a measure of EE. These key variables are hostility, critical comments and emotional over-involvement (Kuipers and Bebbington, 1988). Families which rate high on these variables are said to have a high level of EE. EE is assumed by Leff and his colleagues to be a relatively stable tendency of the family environment which may pre-date the onset of the disorder. An alternative view is that it is the consequence of living with a chronically disabled relative over a long period (Kuipers and Bebbington, 1988). Despite this criticism, studies have now demonstrated the existence of EE in families in a wide range of cultures (Kuipers and Bebbington, 1988). EE has also been shown to vary between families and these variations can be reliably assessed. It also varies within families, being highest around the time of hospital admission; Brown *et al.* (1972) found EE to be high in around 30 per cent of families at the time of admission, dropping to around 14 per cent at follow-up nine-months later. EE has also been shown to predict relapse. Vaughan and Leff (1976) found a 51 per cent relapse rate among patients from high EE families at post-discharge nine-month follow-up in contrast to a 13 per cent relapse rate in patients who returned to low EE families. Although EE does correlate with levels of disturbance, Brown *et al.* (1972) have shown that EE has predictive power over and above the level of patient disturbance. Vaughan and Leff also demonstrated a clear interaction between EE levels and psychotropic medication. For example where there was a high level of EE and non-compliance with medication, the relapse rate was 92 per cent (if the person had more than 35 hours contact with the family per week) and only 15 per cent if there was non-compliance with medication in a low EE family. Therefore it seems reasonable to conclude that EE characterises some relatively stable factor of the family environment. It should not, however, be assumed that only high EE families require or could benefit from family interventions; to do so would deprive many families of help they may need.

The work of Leff and colleagues using EE as the basis for a therapeutic approach contrasts with earlier models of family interventions, for example the work of Laing (Esterson *et al.*, 1965) or Palazzoli *et al.* (1978), in that the emphasis with the EE interventions is not on the cure of schizophrenia, but on the development of appropriate coping strategies within the family and the reduction of relapse. Their programmme (Leff *et al.*, 1985) had three components. First, an education package which was given to relatives in their own homes and consists of four talks on possible causes, symptoms, likely course and treatment. The second element was a relatives support group for both high and low EE families which met on a two-weekly basis. (However, there were problems in maintaining attendance of the low EE family members and this resulted in the professionals running the groups, providing advice on the development of coping strategies that it had intended low EE families would provide.) The final element of the package was the provision of family meetings in the home which had a therapeutic emphasis, borrowing techniques from a range of therapeutic models as seemed appropriate. The number of these sessions varied considerably but averaged around five. An experimental group of patients from high EE families were followed up over a two-year period and their progress compared to a control group of patients who received standard treatment and follow-up. At two-year follow-up Leff *et al.* (1985) were able to show that the relapse rate in the experimental group was significantly lower at 33 per cent, than it was in the group which received standard treatment (75 per cent). The carers support groups run by Kuipers *et al.* (1989) are based on the model and experience gained from this more extensive intervention programme.

A number of programmes in the United States have developed similar approaches to the treatment of families. In the description that follows the differences between these programmes and that of Leff and others will be emphasised. Fallon *et al.* (1984) have developed a system of behavioural family therapy which explicitly rejects the notion of the family as pathogenic and instead sees the family 'as the major resource for the community management of schizophrenia and other major mental illness' (Fallon *et al.*, 1984). In contrast to the Leff programme all patients were kept on oral medication based on the view that long-acting injectables may produce impairment in social functioning whilst having no overall superiority in terms of relapse prevention (Fallon *et al.*, 1978). They also included 'identified patients' in family education sessions and encouraged them to develop expertise in understanding their own illness and symptomatology. However, the major difference was in the nature of the family intervention, where Fallon *et al.* adopted a problem-solving behavioural model which specifically aimed at developing family problem-solving strategies with the aim of reducing the stress experienced by the identified patient. The method was explicitly educational, the therapist teaching a range of problem-solving techniques along with the development of communication skills in the family. The final component consisted of multi-family support groups, based at the hospital, following completion of the family treatment phase.

The family model was compared directly to an individual case management model which also had an educational component and an individually-based problem-solving approach. In a follow-up study of 36 patients who had been assigned either to the family or individual treatment, Fallon *et al.* (1984) were able to show that the family treatment group had a 17 per cent relapse rate compared to that of 83 per cent with the individual treatment group. Improvement was noted on a wide range of variables including clinical state, social functioning, family functioning, tenure in employment or education, and frequency and duration of hospitalisations. As with the Leff studies they found that there was a decrease in the number of critical comments made by relatives. The family programme also was shown to be considerably cheaper than other approaches when a cost-benefit analysis was performed.

The final programme which will be described is that of Hogarty and his colleagues in Pennsylvania (Anderson *et al.*, 1986). In a controlled trial Hogarty *et al.* (1986) looked at the comparative effectiveness of a range of interventions: (1) medication only, (2) family treatment and medication, (3) social skills training and medication and (4) medication, family treatment and social skills training. The aim of the family treatment was to reduce the emotionally laden atmosphere of the family and maintain reasonable expectations of patient performance. A four-phase system of intervention was developed. Phase 1 involved the development of an alliance through twice-weekly sessions during a period of hospitalisation or the acute phase of the illness. In this phase the therapist sought to build the alliance through reducing guilt on the part of family members and also by acting as mediator between the patient and the hospital system. Phase 2 involved one-day 'survival skills' workshops for families in which four or five families came together, were informed about schizophrenia and given the opportunity to share ideas on coping with problems. Relatives were also encouraged to try to develop some mutual support. Phase 3 involved the whole family and patient meeting together fortnightly for six months. This phase was concerned with helping the patient and the family develop appropriate coping skills. In the final phase families are offered the choice of either continuing with the therapy or decreasing their involvement; in either case the possibility of long-term contact with the clinical team remained. The social skills training was geared specifically to helping individuals cope with communication and other problems in a family setting.

At one-year follow-up the results were as impressive as those reported by other studies, with the medication group having a relapse rate of 41 per cent compared to 0 per cent for the full treatment group. Groups that received only family or social skills training had relapse rates of 19 per cent or 20 per cent respectively. Careful measurement of the EE of the families suggested that clear reductions in the level of EE were associated with the most striking therapeutic effects.

Despite a difference in emphasis, programme content and duration all the above programmes have produced positive and strikingly similar results. Strachan (1986) considers the following factors to be common to all three interventions.

*Family therapy techniques* – all adopted a warm, empathetic stance with a strong practical emphasis on coping strategies. All avoid traditional psychodynamic approaches and, indeed, there is evidence to suggest such psychodynamic approaches with families do not work (Kottgen *et al.*, 1984). Strachan (1986) considers the following techniques to be of particular importance.

1 Connecting – each individual was listened to and encouraged to describe their own experiences. In this respect the structured interviews (part of the research protocol) were felt to perform an important therapeutic role through which family members were made to feel valued and important.
2 Reframing – throughout the process the emphasis was on how each family member could help the other; in most programmes the word therapy was generally avoided. At all times attempts were made to reframe family activity in a positive light, e.g. protective rather than over-involved.
3 Focus on current transactions – the focus was very much on current activities and not on the development of symptoms or personality factors. They were concerned not with what was wrong but how difficulties could be overcome.

4 Focus on communication – clarifying communication within the family was an aim of all the programmes.

5 Focus on concrete problem solving – all stressed the development of strategies for enhancing problem solving or coping skills.

*Psychoeducation* – all were concerned directly with the problems of people with schizophrenia and included brief education programmes with specific information about the disorder. Although short, the programmes seemed to have had desired effects and may play an important role in engaging relatives in the programme.

Strachan also notes that there was good compliance with medication in all the studies for both the control and experimental groups. This suggests, that although family programmes may help with medication compliance, ensuring compliance is not a significant means through which the programmes are effective.

The above work has concentrated exclusively on schizophrenia and so questions must remain about its applicability to other groups of long-term mentally ill people. There is evidence to support the value of the EE concept with a range of chronically disabled groups, including depressed and anorectic family members (Tarrier, 1988). However, it is clear that there will need to be adaptations to the education programmes and to the group and family interventions if the techniques are to be more generally applied. It is also probable that the techniques are applicable to a range of carers other than family members. For example, the variable outcomes reported by Linn *et al.* (1980) in a study of Adult Fostering (see Chapter 5) would seem well suited to an intervention based on the methods described above.

Despite the success of these programmes, their uptake in general psychiatric services is patchy. As with all research-orientated programmes there are special conditions which present difficulties with widespread adoption but this alone cannot explain the difficulty. Perhaps mental health professionals' continued ambivalence to the relatives of mentally disabled people in part accounts for this. As well as ambivalence on the part of professionals, families may also reject the offer of a family intervention. They may experience such an offer as blaming in some way, be anxious to avoid contact with services believing the illness to be a 'one-off' or they may simply fail to understand its purpose (Birchwood, 1988). The importance of developing a working alliance with families cannot be over-emphasised. Services may also be limited in the resources available and, as Birchwood points out, all successful programmes have been characterised by a high level of resources.

A number of different approaches are needed to overcome these problems with implementation. First is the acceptance that all families can potentially benefit from such a programme, including those with low EE and those with a family member with a major mental illness other than schizophrenia. This means developing ways of contacting families other than by the identification of high EE families around the time of admission. Birchwood (1988) suggests this requires an education programme on family interventions for all staff, so that they are sensitive to family needs and able to advise or refer them to appropriate services. Programmes will need to be tailored to individual families, taking into account objective as well as subjective burdens and the varying problems presented by different illnesses. An effective, family-based service cannot operate in isolation from other elements of the rehabilitation service, indeed one of the functions of the family service may be to facilitate the use of such services by family members. Non-compliance rates with family interventions can be up to 35 per cent (Birchwood, 1988) and therefore considerable flexibility is required in the development of any programme. Lack of family members should not disbar individuals from the benefits of the programme; other carers can be included in the programme. Finally, the potential benefits of the progammes should be stressed. They include a very wide range of patient benefits, greater client satisfaction, the possibility of increased cost effectiveness and the opportunity to enlist the support and cooperation of families in the move towards comprehensive community-based care.

These programmes are not a panacea for the problems of all families with mentally ill relatives. Creer et al. (1982) highlight a number of areas which require different kinds of input. These include support with meeting self-care and physical care needs perhaps met by domiciliary nursing services; advice on welfare rights and other benefits; respite care (available not just at times of crisis); housing advice or more appropriate accommodation; and the opportunity for both sufferer and relative to engage in separate social activity which may require attendance at a day centre or the provision of a domiciliary sitting service. This serves to emphasise the point already made that family service must be integrated into wider rehabilitation services. The White Paper, *Caring for People,* is explicit in aiming to help families with disabled relatives and a measure of its success will be how effective it is in promoting the coordination of such a wide range of services.

# Chapter Eight

# ASSURING QUALITY SERVICES

## INTRODUCTION

The future of services for long-term mentally ill people is uncertain. The services lack direction and the possible impact of current changes in government legislation is difficult to assess. It is hard to escape the conclusion reached by Shepherd (1989b) that the lot of long-term mentally ill people is to continue to be treated as if they were the indigent poor. Such a view presents a challenge to society which goes far beyond anything which individual service users or providers could resolve. The needs and rights of mentally ill people have to be asserted, both inside and outside the service. Mental health service providers need to form far more effective alliances than they have done so far. Organisations representing families, service users, communities and other professional and political groupings with legitimate interests in mental health services should be welcomed rather than rejected. Politics is not the concern of this book, but without appropriate political action much that has been discussed in this book will be difficult to achieve. Commonalities of interest between these groups, such as adequate resourcing of community services and the proper priority for mentally ill people within the health service, need to be emphasised.

Much of the debate on community care has been sterile and counter-productive. Uncertainty about the direction and pace of change has often stifled opportunities for creative dialogue. A central concern is with the capacity of services and service providers to change and develop as the demands placed on them change. This requires services to develop methods which enable care systems to respond effectively to these demands. Good coordination and management of services is essential. In addition, methods are required which allow for the continual refinement and monitoring of services. Such methods can be grouped under the heading of quality assurance.

## UNDERSTANDING QUALITY

Quality of care and quality of life have been a central concern in mental health services almost since their inception. The origins of the large mental hospitals (the cause of much recent concern about quality of care) lie in public concern with the very poor quality of care provided by the private madhouses of Victorian England. Despite this long-standing concern with quality, no reliable, widely accepted definition of quality has emerged in the field of mental health. Indeed, some authors have suggested that the task should be abandoned, comparing the task of defining quality in mental health to that of defining obscenity in a court of law. Whilst the notion that quality can neither be defined or measured is rejected in this book, the comparison with obscenity is correct in at least one aspect. In both cases, judgements are based on underlying values and there can be no pretence that the situation is otherwise.

Throughout this book a strong emphasis has been placed on the importance of clear principles and goals and it is in relation to such principles that a definition of quality can be developed. Quality is defined as the extent to which the clearly defined principles of a service are translated into service goals which are successfully achieved. Quality assurance refers to any practical attempt to monitor and enhance the quality of a service. Clifford *et al.* (1989), in a book which describes the QUARTZ system, a comprehensive method of quality assurance for mental health services, list a number of different goals for Quality Assurance Systems (QAS). They include facilitating decision making, demonstrating that resources are being used effectively, the demonstration that clients are getting good quality care and developing goals to help change a service. Clifford *et al.* also identify five factors which they consider central to good quality mental health services. These are:

*A clear conception of the task* – including how it is to be achieved. This requires a coherent philosophy of care and appropriate operational policies and what Wolfensberger (1980) has described as 'model coherence'; that is the internal consistency of the theory, goals and practices underlying the service. Staff's practical awareness of the above is of greater importance than written statements.

*Appropriate selection and delivery of care* – this concerns the organisation and content of care. Staff awareness of the range of approaches to the understanding and treatment of mental health problems is of importance, as is ensuring continuity of care

*Attention to the client's quality of life* – this is concerned with those aspects of the care environment not usually covered by the treatment function. It is concerned with the management practices of a setting and in particular with the nature of staff–client interactions.

*Cohesive multi-disciplinary functioning* – this is necessary to meet the wide range of client needs identified in mental health. Effective team functioning built around a clear understanding of team members' roles is of importance, as is good communication and cooperation.

*An integrated structure to the overall service* – priorities should be identified and resourced appropriately. Elements of the service should be coordinated and there should be effective links between clinicians and managers.

## METHODS OF QUALITY ASSURANCE

Shaw (1986) has set out the basic elements of any quality assurance programme. This involves, first, the selection of a focus for the programme, followed by the identification and monitoring of key indicators. Levels of practice are then identified and the desired aims are compared with current performance. Finally, on the basis of observations made, action is taken to enhance or maintain quality. Quality assurance is then a cyclical process of assessment followed by intervention followed by a reassessment (see Figure 8.1)

Another important distinction is that drawn by Donabedian

136

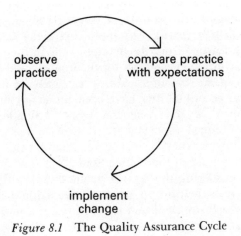

*Figure 8.1* The Quality Assurance Cycle

(1966) between structure (or input), process and outcome, providing a useful framework for the organisation of the information collected as part of any quality assurance programme. Structure is concerned with the basic resources that a service has at its disposal, including the physical, the financial and the staff resources. The other main structural or input variable is the clients who use the service. Process variables are concerned with the activities of a service including the method of organisation of a service and the content and style of service delivered. Outcome is concerned with the effect that a service has on its clients, not just in narrow clinical terms, but also in terms of its impact on the clients' quality of life. Although of central importance, outcome is difficult to measure, particularly in rehabilitation where concepts of 'cure' are of little value. Donabedian's model is limited by the difficulty that often arises in understanding the precise relationship between the three variables. For example, did the improved client outcome demonstrated in one setting occur as a result of the addition of another staff member, was it because of the new system of case coordination that was introduced at the same time, or was it the result of some interaction between the two? Understanding such distinctions is important because it may help decide whether other services need new methods of case coordination, more staff or both.

Quality assurances methods in mental health have developed much more rapidly in the United States in the past 15 years than they have done in this country. Zusman (1988) and Stricker and Rodriguez (1988) provide very useful overviews. There is much that can be learned from the developments in the United States but the very different methods for the funding and organisation of services mean that this learning can only be indirect. Cost control and accountability have been the major driving forces behind much of the American work (Lalonde, 1982) and although of central importance to the provision of services in the United Kingdom they have not yet attained the pre-eminent position they hold in the United States.

When considering the detailed methods available for quality assurance it is helpful to draw a distinction between those methods which use the existing resources of a setting (internal review) and those which use resources beyond those available to the immediate care setting (external review). In the discussion that follows the methods available will be summarised and where possible examples from existing practice will be described.

## Internal review

Methods of internal review are rooted in the everyday practice of a setting. Much valuable quality assurance is done through case conferences, ward rounds, and staff support groups and this existing resource should not be forgotten in the development of any QAS. The strength of these methods lies in their concern with the live issues of clinical care. At their most effective they can place an appropriate emphasis on input, process and outcome variables. As well as monitoring the quality of service provided they also allow for effective implementation of change to further enhance quality. Such systems can, however, be rather inward looking, focusing on specific issues of the moment rather than general trends in service development. To some extent this can be counteracted by the introduction of more formalised systems for organising the review, e.g. the development of a Goal Attainment Scaling system to aid in the monitoring of in-patients such as is described by Guy and Moore (1982). Computer-based systems or registers which aim at coordinating the work of a number of professionals (Whitehead, 1987) can also been seen as quality assurance systems. Methods of internal review tend to neglect the relationship of the setting in which they operate to that of the overall service and this can be a major deficit. Finally, they are notorious for neglecting difficult issues, a tendency which can be overcome by the introduction of an external facilitator.

Supervision of staff by more senior members or the introduction of systems such as the Individual Performance Review, are examples of individually-based procedures which can lead to improvements in service quality. They can provide effective methods for identifying necessary changes in staff behaviour. At times they fail to consider the wider context, leaving the possibility open that such changes may not be in the interests of the service. Quality Circles (Robson, 1982) have an explicit focus on service quality and are commonly found in industry. They consist of small groups of staff drawn from the same workplace and are usually established and run by a local coordinator according to a pre-determined problem-solving format. The explicit focus on quality helps with the implementation of change but they too tend to focus on internal matters and so ignore the wider service context. Blunden and Beyer (1987) describe an interesting variant of the Quality Circle called a Quality Assurance Group in which staff members from a setting meet with external stakeholders such as service users, family members, and representatives from other services. The format has much in common with quality circles but demands more effective skills and management on behalf of some of the participants to work effectively. Quality assurance groups have the advantage of focusing on links with external agencies as well as the internal workings of the setting.

*External review*

Inspectorates

These are one of the most commonly employed methods of external review. Within this country the Health Advisory Service (HAS) has a key role in inspecting and promoting good practice in psychiatric services. It operates through visits of three to six weeks duration to health districts. Such visits provide a useful external perspective and can provide a valuable impetus for change. However, all too often, the action following on from a HAS visit is concerned to produce changes which will satisfy the next inspection rather than bring about postive long-term improvement in service quality. The Mental Health Act Commission performs a similar function to that of the HAS but its brief is limited to the care of patients formally detained under the Mental Health Act. Such bodies are often greeted with much suspicion by staff and the defensive posture this generates often works against progress. The White Paper, *Caring for People*, places great stress on the role of independent local authority inspection units. It remains to be seen whether they will be able to escape from a troubleshooting or policing role to one concerned with the promotion of quality services.

### Research evaluations

This commonly used method of external review stresses outcome (sometimes at the expense of process measures) and introduces an element of objectivity. Both are important elements missing from many other methods. Usually evaluations are 'one-off' exercises designed to show whether or not a service is effective. This leads to many problems with the implementation of change, in part due to the considerable anxiety that can be generated. The technical and resource demands of many research programmes also mean that they are usually unsuited to continuing review. Even where good outcome has been identified it is often difficult to specify what are the important processes of care which have been responsible for the good outcome. Of course the reverse is true with regard to the process of care; there is a dearth of evidence demonstrating a causal link between good quality of care and positive outcomes.

### Standard setting

This approach is one of the commonest methods of quality assurance in the United States (Zusman, 1988). It is also in common use among certain professional groups (for example, nurses), particularly in the field of physical medicine. Typically this involves the setting of a standard to be met in the care of a particular client group. Deviation from this standard usually involves some form of further review (for example, peer review).

140

In the United Kingdom a number of methods are in use, including the PASS system based on the theory of normalisation (Wolfensberger and Glenn, 1973), the checklist provided by Good Practices in Mental Health (1988) in their publication *Treated Well* (which is concerned with the care of psychiatric in-patients) and the 'Model Standards Questionnaires' developed by Lavender (1987). Such systems have the major advantage of providing an external yardstick against which the performance of a service can be assessed. Systems such as PASS also pay attention to wider service issues. They can lead to explicit recommendations about action to be taken to improve performance.

However, there are considerable problems with these systems, for example, with the definition of criteria, with whether or not maximum or minimum standards should be adopted and their general lack of flexibility. Maximum standards may lead to excessively critical feedback. Minimum standards may lead to low expectations and fail to provide indications for future developments. Perhaps the greatest drawback of all the models is the absence of any outcome data, the emphasis being on process and input data. As a result it is not possible to be certain that the care practices recommended will lead to better outcomes. In the United States this has led accreditation bodies responsible for the setting of standards to move away from process measures towards an exclusive reliance on outcome measures. It is, however, anticipated that this will cause considerable problems in the mental health field (Fauman, 1989). In addition, such methods often require considerable training and skill if they are to be successfully implemented. Despite these drawbacks they can be effective. A good example of their use is provided by Lavender (1987). Using his Model Standards Questionnaires (which cover four areas: treatment practices, management practices, community contact and the physical environment) he was able to demonstrate that carefully prepared positive feedback from specific questionnaires produced changes in care practices in the desired direction.

## Peer review systems

Such systems are concerned with the review of the care received by individual clients. They comprise the major model for quality assurance in the United States and are common in many general medical settings. The care of individual clients is reviewed by a panel of experienced professional peers who are independent of the individual or group responsible for the delivery of care. The system is based on the concept of good professional practice and is concerned directly with both client outcome and the overall functioning of the care system in relation to individual clients. Problems often arise when developing criteria for selection of cases for peer review. Typically selection is triggered when an agreed standard is not met (for example, all individuals in a certain diagnostic group should normally receive no more than eight out-patient appointments) or certain events occur (e.g. a suicide). Inevitably such systems tend to focus on service failures and there is less opportunity to commend good practice. It should also be pointed out that there is no evidence that peer review systems have of themselves brought about positive changes in service quality (Sechrest and Rosenblatt, 1988).

## Consumer feedback

This is a recent development in mental health, but like Quality Circles has its origins in industry. In the field of mental health the Quality of Life Interview developed by Lehman (1983) is amongst the best known. It reviews objective and subjective satisfaction in eight life areas: living situation, leisure activity, family relations, social relations, work, health, finance and personal safety. Such instruments have been used in the detailed evaluation of a number of service settings. For example, Simpson *et al.* (1989) used the Lehman scale to evaluate the quality of life of residents in a hospital hostel compared to that found in a number of group homes or an in-patient unit. Other less complex scales are described by Baker and Intagliata (1981). All satisfaction measures suffer from the tendency of those surveyed to rate high whatever the circumstances; Baker and Intagliata report average satisfaction ratings of around 75 per cent. Whilst such feedback may be good for morale or public relations it is not very informative. They are probably only useful when repeatedly administered in the same setting. Lehman's (1983) work also demonstrates another problem with satisfaction measures, that of using global ratings to measure complex dimensions of care. He reported on the importance placed on items like finance, personal safety and family relations by residents of a Californian Board and Lodge home. This contrasted strongly with the emphasis placed by professionals on various forms of treatment. It is possible that these distinctions would have been lost if a global construct of quality of life had been used. A further problem concerns the level at which such information should be collated. At the direct care level personal knowledge may inhibit the data collection process whilst at a more senior level it may be too abstract to promote appropriate interventions.

## Advocacy

The term covers a wide range of activities, all of which are concerned with strengthening the voice of service users in determining the provision of services. Barker and Peck (1988) describe numerous examples of advocacy schemes. Essentially they fall into two broad groups, those concerned with group activity and those concerned with individual care. The establishment of a Mental Health Forum is a relatively common form of group activity. The membership consists of current and past users of mental health services in the local area. In some cases they may also involve interested professionals. With adequate resources and funding such groups can make a real contribution to improve service quality. For them to be effective professionals must consult and involve such organisations in meaningful ways and avoid token gestures. Their greatest difficulty seems to be with ensuring their own survival, Harris (1989) provides an interesting description of the struggles leading to the establishment of one local forum in Islington, London. Patients' Councils, which function in settings such as an in-patient units or a day hospitals, are another form of group advocacy. They function to express client views on the care delivered in the areas in which they are based. Other projects, such as the Legal Advice Project based at Springfield Hospital in London, have developed with much more narrow and specific briefs.

There are also a variety of individual advocacy models. These include self-advocacy, where the individual acts as advocate on their own behalf, often after a period of training by a body established specifically for that purpose. Alternatively an organisation may train volunteers specifically to act as advocates for people who, for a variety of reasons, are unable to represent themselves. Some services employ paid advocates who advise on legal, welfare and other rights as well representing users in their demands for services. In other areas agencies have been established to coordinate the activities of various advocacy groups, for example, the Nottingham Advocacy Group which coordinates advocacy activities for mentally ill people in Nottingham. Individual advocacy methods are a potentially powerful force for service development, but care must be taken that advocacy does not turn into antagonism.

Consultancy

This involves the appointment of an external agent to advise on the solution of a problem in the working of an existing service or the establishment of a new service. Usually it concentrates on management issues in care delivery and is almost limitless in its flexibility. Invariably it is a 'one-off' exercise and this constrains the degree to which the recommended changes can be implemented and followed through. It is probable that its effectiveness is largely determined by an organisation's willingness to work with the consultants.

## IMPLEMENTING A QUALITY ASSURANCE SYSTEM

All the various methods described above have something to offer as quality assurance systems. As with most things in rehabilitation no one method is sufficient, but as long as its limitations are acknowledged and the limits imposed by resources and the capacity of the local services for change are recognised, most methods can be used as a basis for further development. It is usually easiest to establish a new system where there are enthusiastic local supporters and existing good practices to build on and develop. Whether starting with the development of a simple rating scale for client satisfaction or the implementation of a comprehensive system like QUARTZ (Clifford *et al.*, 1989) the following guidelines should be borne in mind even if it is not always possible to comply with the suggested course of action. Being aware of an organisation's limited ability to change can lead to the development of a far more effective quality assurance system than unrealistic and omnipotent theorising. Far too many quality assurance programmes have ignored this vital point and

are appropriately characterised as 'technical successes but organisational disasters' (Forquer and Anderson, 1982).

### Guidelines on the implementation of Quality Assurance Systems

1 Monitoring and enhancement should be compatible – simply
measuring something will not produce change in the desired
direction. Even with the simplest systems thought must be given
as to how the information obtained will facilitate change. An
essential element in achieving the desired change is that staff
have some ownership of the system which is to be implemented.
Just as participation in management improves the quality of care
in settings (Raynes *et al.*, 1979) so participation in the development of quality assurance programmes improves their effectiveness.

2 Elements of both internal and external review are desirable –
staff must play a central role in any quality assurance system and
yet care must be taken to see that the system does not become too
insular. Open systems are the healthiest and an appropriate
balance must be struck between these two elements.

3 The method must include elements of objectivity – objectivity
is not achieved through repetitive form filling. Clarity of purpose
and explicit guidelines on areas to be reviewed and the methods
by which this can be achieved, are of great importance.

4 Stated goals and priorities are required – clearly stated goals
and priorities are the context in which effective quality assurance
systems operate. Some quality assurance work can be done to
determine to what extent the goals of a service are understood.
However, without clear goals no quality assurance system can
function effectively in the long term. The need for clarity in this
area highlights the importance of management ownership and
support for any quality assurance system.

5 Management commitment should reflect management practice
– this commitment can be demonstrated in a number of ways.
Quality assurance systems must be adequately resourced. The
impact of QAS at all levels of the service system must be
anticipated and the means by which information and decision-
making systems operate developed to promote quality. There is
no more demoralising experience for staff than to be encouraged

to look at improving service quality and then find their suggestions blocked by the lack of adequate management response.
Without the acceptance of the need for such systems neither
direct care staff or managers should commit themselves to quality
assurance programmes.

6 A comprehensive approach is desirable – quality is multi-
faceted and there is a danger that focusing on too narrow or
specific aspects of practice will limit the ability of the service to
identify opportunities for growth and development. Systems
should consider any monitoring in relation to the input, process
and outcome variables that characterise the service. Where a
limited or narrow focus is chosen for detailed review it is helpful
to set this in an appropriate context, perhaps through the
production of an annual report.

7 Outcome must be considered – meaningful outcome data is
difficult to collect and often more difficult to interpret as so many
variables affect outcome in mental health services. The advantages and disadvantages of satisfaction data, relatively simple
'outcome' data to collect, have already been discussed. To be of
real value a range of outcome measures must be collected.

8 The importance of user participation – considerable stress
should be placed on the involvement of users in QAS. Services
should aim to make users more than passive respondents to
questionnaires. There should be mechanisms by which users can
comment on the development, purpose and implementation of
the system; such a dialogue will, for many services, represent a
move forward in terms of quality assurance.

9 Staff anxieties must be addressed – whatever the complexity of
a quality system it cannot work without the support of the staff
concerned. This means the staff need to develop ownership of the
system and their anxieties about the system addressed. Forquer
and Anderson (1982) provide a useful overview of the anxieties
that such systems generate and the consequences of ignoring
them. They argue that many quality assurance systems fail due to
staff resistance and argue that the process of implementation
must operate in parallel with an exploration and resolution of
staff anxieties. Staff anxieties fall into three areas:

1 Self concerns which include the demands on paperwork generated by a QAS, the premium it places on administration or cost

146

control over clinical practice and the threat to jobs implicit in any monitoring system.

2 Task concerns which include such criticisms as the adequacy of the rating systems developed, the method for reviewing outcome data or the applicability of the system to certain client groups.

3 Impact concerns which include the need to review training procedures and the possibility of changing aspects of the settings overall goals.

Forquer and Anderson argue that the above concerns must be dealt with in discussion with staff. They argue these discussions should move in parallel with the implementation process and where this does not happen implementation will fail. Before any use of the QAS is made, self concerns must be discussed. In the initial stages of implementation task concerns will be prominent. Finally, as the QAS is further developed and refined, impact concerns become the primary focus of discussion. Although the structure is a little rigid it does provide a useful framework for considering staff concerns. In addition to staff discussion Forquer and Anderson suggest that for successful implementation adequate resources at the financial, staff, administrative and emotional level are required. Not least among these is the requirement that any staff involved are properly trained in its use.

## CONCLUSION

Achieving real improvements in service quality will be a key indicator by which the success of rehabilitation services for long-term mentally ill people will be measured. Community-based services must provide, and be seen to provide, better quality services than the large mental hospitals. To achieve this, services have to be adequately resourced and integrated into a comprehensive system of health and social care which is responsive to individual needs and offers real choice to its users. This means a partnership has to be established between service users, their carers and service providers which recognises and values the contribution of all concerned. Quality assurance programmes are one method by which this partnership can be established.

# REFERENCES

Allyon, T. and Azrin, N.H. (1968) *The Token Economy: A Motivational System for Therapy and Rehabilitation*, Appleton Century Crofts, New York.

Anderson, C.M., Reiss, D.J. and Hogarty, G.E. (1986) *Schizophrenia in the Familiy. A Practioners Guide to Psychoeducation and Management*, Guildford Press, New York.

Anthony, W.A. and Farkas, M. (1982) 'A client-outcome planning model for assessing psychiatric rehabilitation interventions', *Schizophrenia Bulletin* 8, 13–38.

Anthony, W.A., Pierce, R.M., Cohen, M.R. and Cannon, J.R. (1981) *The Skills of Diagnostic Planning: Psychiatric Rehabilitation Pratice Series*, University Park Press, Baltimore.

Apte, R.Z. (1968) 'Halfway Houses: A New Dilemma in Social Care', *Occasional Papers on Social Administration*, G. Bell and Sons Ltd, London.

Audit Commission (1986) *Making a Reality of Community Care*, HMSO, London.

Bacharach, L.L. (1983) 'Concepts and Issues in Deinstitutionalization', in Barofsky, I. and Budson, R.D. (eds) *The Chronic Psychiatric Patient in the Community*, MTP Press Ltd, Lancaster.

Bacharach, L.L. (1988) 'Defining chronic mental illness: a concept paper', *Hospital and Community Psychiatry* 39, 383–8.

Backer, T.E., Liberman, R.P. and Kuehnel, T.G. (1986) 'Dissemination and adoption of innovative psychosocial interventions', *Journal of Consulting and Clinical Psychology* 54, 111–18.

Baker, R. and Hall, J.N. (1983) *Rehab: Rehabilitation Evaluation*, Vine Publishing, Aberdeen.

Baker, F. and Intagliata, J, (1981) 'Quality of life in the evaluation of community support', *Evaluation and Programme Planning* 8 (1), 69–79.

Balderessarini, R.J. (1983) 'Clinical Psychopharmacology and Side Effects of Anti-Psychotic and Mood Stabilizing Drugs used in the Treatment of Psychiatric Patients with Chronic or Recurrent

Disorders', in Barofsky, I. and Budson, R.D. (eds) *The Chronic Psychiatric Patient in the Community*, MTP Press Ltd, Lancaster.

Barker, I. and Peck, E. (1988) *Power in Strange Places: User Empowerment in Mental Health Services*, Good Practices in Mental Health, London.

Bateson, G., Jackson, D., Haley, J. and Weakland, J.(1956) 'Towards a theory of schizophrenia', *Behavioural Science* 1, 251-64.

Baxter, E. and Hopper, K. (1984) 'Troubled on the Streets; The Mentally Disabled Homeless Poor', in Talbot, J.A. (ed.) *The Chronic Mental Patient; Five Years Later*, Grune and Stratton, New York.

Bayliss, E. (1987) *Housing: The Foundation of Community Care*, MIND and the National Federation of Housing Associations, London.

Beard, J., Probst, R. and Malamud, T.J. (1982) 'The Fountain House model of psychiatric rehabilitation', *Psychosocial Rehabilitation Journal* 5, 47-53.

Bellack, A.S. and Hersen, M. (1988) *Behavioural Assessment: A Practical Handbook*, Pergamon, New York.

Bender, M.P. and Pilling, S. (1985) 'A study of variables associated with under-attendance at a psychiatric day centre', *Psychological Medicine* 15, 395-401.

Bennett, D.H. (1978) 'Social Forms of Psychiatric Treatment', in Wing, J.K. (ed.) *Schizophrenia: Towards a New Synthesis*, Academic Press, London.

Bennett, D.H. (1983) 'The Historical Development of Rehabilitation Services', in Watts, F.N. and Bennett, D.H. (eds) *Theory and Practice of Psychiatric Rehabilitation*, John Wiley, London.

Birchwood, M. (1988) 'Families and the management of schizophrenia', paper presented at Rehabilitation Conference, Oxford, December 1988.

Birchwood, M. and Smith, J. (1986) 'Schizophrenia', in Orford, J. (ed.) *Coping with Disorder in the Family*, Croom Helm, London.

Birchwood, M., Smith, J., Macmillan, F., Hogg, B., Prasad, R., Harvey, C. and Bering, S. (1989) 'Predicting relapse in schizophrenia: the development and implementation of an early signs monitoring system using patients and families as observers, a preliminary investigation', *Psychological Medicine* 19, 649-56.

Blake, R., Millard, D.W. and Roberts, J.P. (1984) 'Therapeutic community principles in an integrated local authority mental health service', *International Journal of Theraputic Communities* 5, 243-73.

Blunden, R. and Beyer, S. (1987) 'Pursuing Quality: a practical approach, in Ward, L. (ed.) *Getting Better All the Time?* Kings Fund Centre, London.

Bond, G.R., Miller, L.D., Krumweid, M.H.A. and Ward, R.S. (1988) 'Assertive case management in three CMHCs: a controlled study', *Hospital and Community Psychiatry* 39, 411-18.

Borland, A., McRae, J. and Lycan, C. (1989) 'Outcomes of five years intensive case management', *Hospital and Community Psychiatry* 40, 369-76.

Bradshaw, J. (1972) 'A Taxonomy of Social Need', in McLachan, G. (ed.) *Problems and Progress in Medical Care*, Oxford University Press, Oxford.

Brewin, C.R., Wing, J.K., Mangen, S.P., Brugha, T.S. and McCarthy, B. (1987) 'Principles and practices of measuring needs of the long-term mentally ill: The MRC needs for care assessment', *Psychological Medicine* 17, 971–81.

Brewin, C.R., Wing, J.K., Mangen, S.P., Brugha, T.S., McCarthy, B. and Lesage, A. (1988) 'Needs for care among the long-term mentally ill: a report from the Camberwell High Contact Study', *Psychological Medicine* 18, 457–68.

Brim, O.G. and Wheeler, S. (1966) *Socialization after Childhood: Two Essays*, John Wiley, New York.

Brost, M. and Johnston, T. (1982) *Getting to Know You – One Approach to Service Assessment and Planning for Individuals with Disabilities*, Wisconsin Council of Developmental Disabilities, Madison, Wisconsin.

Brown, G.W. and Harris, T. (1978) *Social Origins of Depression*, Tavistock Publications, London.

Brown, G.W., Monck, G.M., Carstairs, G. and Wing, J.K. (1962) 'Influence of family life on the course of schizophrenic illness', *British Journal of Social and Preventative Medicine* 16, 55–68.

Brown, G.W., Birley, J.L.T. and Wing, J.K. (1972) 'Influence of family life on the course of schizophrenic disorders: a replication', *British Journal of Psychiatry* 121, 241–58.

Budson, R.D. (1983) 'Residential Care of the Chronically Mentally Ill', in Barofsky, I. and Budson, R.D. (eds) *The Chronic Psychiatric Patient in the Community*, MTP Press Ltd, Lancaster.

Budson, R.D. and Jolley, R.E. (1978) 'A crucial factor in community program success: the extended psychosocial kinship system', *Schizophrenia Bulletin* 4, 384–98.

Carling, P.J. and Ridgeway, P. (1989) 'A Psychiatric Rehabilitation Approach to Housing', in Anthony, W. and Farkas, M (eds) *Psychiatric Rehabilitation: Programs and Practices*, Johns Hopkins University Press, Baltimore.

Challis, D.J. and Davis, B.P. (1986) *Case Management in Community Care*, Gower, London.

Christie-Brown, J.R.W., Ebringer, L. and Freedman, K.S. (1977) 'A survey of long-stay psychiatric population: implications for community services', *Psychological Medicine* 7, 113–26.

Clark, D. (1977) *The Therapeutic Community*, Tavistock Publications, London.

Clifford, P. (1987) *The Community Placement Questionnaire*, National Unit for Research and Development in Psychiatry, London.

Clifford, P. (1988) 'Out of the Cuckoo's Nest: The Move of T2 Ward from Bexley Hospital to 215 Sydenham Road', in Lavender, A. and Holloway, F. (eds) *Community Care in Practice*, Wiley, London.

Clifford, P. and Craig, T. (1989) *The Development of Case Management*

*Systems: a proposed inter-agency initiative*, National Unit for Psychiatric Research and Development, London.

Clifford, P. and Wolfson, P. (1989) *Functional Assessment of Care Environments (FACE)*, National Unit for Psychiatric Research and Development, London.

Clifford, P., Lavender, A., Leiper, R. and Pilling, S. (1989) *Assuring Quality in Mental Health Services: The QUARTZ System*, Free Associations/RDP, London.

Conolly, J. (1847; republished 1967) *The Construction and Government of the Lunatic Asylums and Hospitals for the Insane*, Dawsons of Pall Mall, London.

Cornes, P., Alderman, J., Cumella, S., Harradance, J., Huttton, D. and Tebbutt, A.G. (1982) *Employment Rehabilitation: the aims and achievements of a service for disabled people*, Manpower Services Commission, HMSO, Sheffield.

Creer, C., Sturt, E. and Wykes, T. (1982) 'The role of relatives', in Wing, J.K. (ed.) 'Long-term community care: experience in a London borough', *Psychological Medicine Monograph Supplement 2.*

Davis, A. (1985) 'Who wants day care?'. Paper presented at 'Alternatives in Day Care' Conference, King's Fund Centre, London.

DHSS (1975) *Better Services for the Mentally Ill*, HMSO, London.

DHSS (1979) *Organizational and Management Problems of Mental Illness Hospitals*, HMSO, London.

DHSS (1989) *Caring for People*, HMSO, London.

Donabedian, A. (1966) 'Evaluating the quality of medical care', *Millbank Memorial Fund Quarterly* 44, 166-203.

Donaldson, S., Greenblatt, A.J. and Balderessarini, R.J. (1983) 'Pharmacologic treatment of schizophrenia: a progress report', *Schizophrenia Bulletin* 9, 504-27.

Dwyer, W.G. (1977) *Team Building*, Addison Wesly, Reading, Mass.

Early, D.F. and Magnus, R.V. (1968) 'The industrial therapy organization (Bristol) 1960-1965', *British Journal of Psychiatry* 114, 335-6.

Edwards, C. and Carter, J. (1979) 'Day Services and the Mentally Ill', in Wing, J.K. and Olsen, R. (eds) *Community Care for the Mentally Disabled*, Oxford University Press, Oxford.

Embleton, C. (1985) 'Day care, a focus for natural support systems'. Paper presented at 'Alternatives in Day Care' Conference, King's Fund Centre, London.

Esterson, A., Cooper, D.G. and Laing, R.D (1965) 'Results of family orientated therapy with hospitalised schizophrenics', *British Medical Journal* 2, 1462-5.

Fallon, I.R.H. and Talbot, R.E. (1982) 'Achieving the goals of day treatment', *Journal of Nervous and Mental Diseases* 170, 279-85.

Fallon, I.R.H., Watt, D.C. and Shepherd, M. (1978) 'The social outcome of patients in a trial of long-term continuation therapy in schizophrenia: Pimozide vs. Fluphenazine', *Psychological Medicine* 8, 265-74.

Fallon, I.R.H., Boyd, J.L. and McGill, C.W. (1984) *Family Care of Schizophrenia*, Guildford Press, New York.

Fauman, M. (1989) 'Quality assurance monitoring in psychiatry',*American Journal of Psychiatry* 146, 1121-30.

Floyd, M. (1984) 'The employment problems of people disabled by schizophrenia' *Journal of Social and Occupational Medicine* 34, 93-5.

Flynn, R. and Nitsch, K. (1980) (eds) *Normalisation, Social Integration and Community Services*, University Press, Baltimore.

Ford, M., Goddard, C. and Landsdall-Welfare, R. (1987) 'The dismantling of the mental hospital: Glenside Hospital surveys 1960-1985' *British Journal of Psychiatry* 151, 479-85.

Forquer, S.L. and Anderson, T.B. (1982) 'A concerns-based approach to the implementation of quality assurance systems' *Quality Review Bulletin* (April) 14-19.

Freud, S. (1930) *Civilisation and its Discontents*, Penguin, London.

Fromm-Reichman, F. (1948) 'Notes on the development of treatment of schizophrenics by psychoanalytic therapy', *Psychiatry* 11, 263-73.

Garety, P.A. (1988) 'Housing', in Lavender, A. and Holloway, F. (eds) *Community Care in Practice*, John Wiley, London.

Garety, P.A. and Morris, I. (1984) 'A new unit for long-stay patients: organization, attitude and quality of care', *Psychological Medicine* 14, 183-92.

Garety, P.A., Afele, H.K. and Issacs, A.D. (1988) 'A hostel-ward for new long-stay patients. The careers of the first 10 years' residents', *Psychiatric Bulletin* 12, 183-6.

Georgiades, N. and Philmore, L. (1975) 'The Myth of the Hero-Innovator and Alternative Stratergies for Organizational Change', in Kiernan, C. and Woodford, P. (eds) *Behaviour Modification with the Severely Retarded*, Associated Scientific Publications, New York.

Goffman, I. (1961) *Asylums*, Penguin, London.

Goldberg, D.B., Bridges, K., Cooper, W., Hyde, C. Sterling, C. and Wyatt, R. (1985) 'Douglas House: a new type of hostel for chronic psychiatric patients', *British Journal of Psychiatry* 147, 383-8.

Good Practices in Mental Health (1988) *Treated Well: A Code of Practice for Psychiatric Hospitals*, Good Practices in Mental Health, London.

Grad, J. and Sainsbury, P. (1968) 'The effects that patients have on their families in a community care and a control psychiatric service - a two year follow-up', *British Journal of Psychiatry* 114, 265-78.

Griffin Francell, C., Conn, V.S. and Gray, D.P. (1988) 'Families' perception of burden of care for chronically mentally ill relatives', *Hospital and Community Psychiatry* 12, 1296-300.

Griffiths, R. (1988) *Community Care: An Agenda for Action*, HMSO, London.

Gudeman, J.E., Dickey, B. and Evans, A. (1985) 'Four year assessment of a day hospital-inn program as an alternative to hospitalization', *American Journal of Psychiatry* 142, 1330-3.

Guy, M.E. and Moore, L.S. (1982) 'The goal attainment scale for psychiatric in-patients', *Quality Review Bulletin* (June), 19-29.

Hall, J.N. (1980) 'Ward ratings scales for long-stay patients: a review', *Psychological Medicine* 10, 277-88.

Hall, J.N. (1983) 'Ward-based Rehabilitation Programmes', in Watts, F.N. and Bennett, D. (eds) *Theory and Practice of Psychiatric Rehabilitation*, John Wiley, London.

Hall, J.N. (1984) 'Issues in Assessment', in Simpson, S., Higson, P., Holland, R., McBrien, J., Williams, J. and Henneman, L. (eds) *Facing the Challenge*, British Association for Behavioural Psychotherapy, Rossendale.

Hall, J.N., Baker, R.D. and Hutchinson, K. (1977) 'A controlled evaluation of token economy procedures with chronic psychiatric patients', *Behaviour Research and Therapy* 15, 261-83.

Hamid, W.A. and McCarthy, M. (1989) 'Community psychiatric care for homeless people in inner London', *Health Trends* 21, 67-71.

Harding, C.M., Strauss, J.S., Hafez, H. and Liberman, P.B. (1987) 'Work and mental illness 1. Towards an integration of the rehabilitation process', *Journal of Nervous and Mental Diseases* 175, 317-26.

Harris, B. (1989) *The Islington Forum*, Good Practices in Mental Health, London.

Harris, M.H. and Bergman, H.C. (1988) 'Misconceptions about the use of case management services by the chronic mentally ill: a utilization analysis', *Hospital and Community Psychiatry* 39, 1276-80.

Herz, M.J. (1982) 'Research overview in day treatment', *International Journal of Partial Hospitalization* 1, 33-44.

Herz, M.J., Endicot, J. and Spitzer, R.L. (1977) 'Brief hospitalization: a two year follow-up', *American Journal of Psychiatry* 134, 502-6.

Hirsch, S.R. (1982) 'Medication and the Physical Treatment of Schizophrenia', in Wing, J.K. and Wing, L. (eds) *Handbook of Psychiatry Volume 3. Psychoses of Uncertain Origin*, Cambridge University Press, Cambridge.

Hogarty, G.E., Schooler, N.R., Ulrich, R., Musscare, F., Fero, P and Herron, E. (1974) 'Fluphenazine and social therapy in the aftercare of schizophrenia', *Archives of General Psychiatry* 36, 1283-94.

Hogarty, G.E., Anderson, C.M., Reiss, D.J., Kornblith, S.J., Greenwald, D.P., Javna, C.D., Madonia, M.J. and the EPCIS Schizophrenia Research Group (1986) 'Family psycho-education, social skills training and maintenance chemotherapy in the aftercare treatment of schizophrenia: 1. One year effects of a controlled study on relapse and expressed emotion', *Archives of General Psychiatry* 43, 633-42.

Holloway, F. (1988a) 'Prescribing for the long-term mentally ill - a study of treatment practices', *British Journal of Psychiatry* 152, 511-15.

Holloway, F. (1988b) 'Day Care and Community Support', in Lavender, A. and Holloway, F. (eds) *Community Care in Practice*, John Wiley, London.

Holloway, F. (1989) 'Psychiatric day care: the users perspective'. Paper submitted for publication.

Hoult, J. and Reynoulds, I. (1984) 'Schizophrenia: a comparative trial of community orientated and hospital orientated psychiatric care', *Acta Psychiatrica Scandanavia* 69, 359-72.

Howatt, J., Bates, P., Pidgeon, J. and Shepperson, G. (1988) 'The Development of Residential Accommodation in the Community', in Lavender, A. and Holloway, F. (eds) *Community Care in Practice*, John Wiley, London.

Hyde, C., Bridges, K., Goldberg, D., Lowson, K., Sterling, C. and Faragher, B. (1987) 'The evaluation of a hostel ward – a controlled study using modified cost-benefit analysis', *British Journal of Psychiatry* 151, 805–12.

Jacobs, H.E., Kardashian, S., Keel Keinberg, R., Ponder, R. and Simpson, A.R. (1984) 'A skills orientated model for facilitating employment among psychiatrically disabled persons', *Rehabilitation Counselling Bulletin* (December) 87–96.

Jahoda, M. (1981) 'Work, employment and unemployment: values, theories and approaches in social research', *American Psychologist* 36, 184–91.

Kanter, J. (1989) 'Clinical case management: definitions, principles and components', *Hospital and Community Psychiatry* 40, 361–8.

Kazdin, A.E. (1975) *Behaviour Modification in Applied Settings* The Dorsey Press, Illinois.

Kendell, R.E. (1989) 'The future of Britain's mental hospitals', *British Medical Journal* 299, 1237–8.

King, R, Raynes, N. and Tizard, J. (1971) *Patterns of Residential Care* Routledge & Kegan Paul, London.

King's Fund (1987) *The Need for Asylum in Society for the Mentally Ill or Infirm*, King's Fund Centre, London.

Kingsley, S. and Towell, D. (1988) 'Planning for High-Quality Local Services', in Lavender, A. and Holloway, F. (eds) *Community Care in Practice*, John Wiley, London.

Kiresuk, T.M. and Sherman, R.E. (1968) 'Goal attainment scaling: a general method for evaluating comprehensive community mental health programs', *Community Mental Health Journal* 4, 443–53.

Kottgen, C., Sonnichsen, I., Mollenhauer, K. and Jurth, R. (1984) 'Group therapy with the families of schizophrenic patients: results of the Hamburg Camberwell Family Interview study', *International Journal of Family Psychiatry* 5, 83–94.

Kuipers, L. and Bebbington, P. (1988) 'Expressed emotion research in schizophrenia: theoretical and clinical implications', *Psychological Medicine* 18, 893–909.

Kuipers, L., McCarthy, B., Hurry, J. and Harper, R. (1989) 'Counselling the relatives of the long-term adult mentally ill, II. A low cost support model', *British Journal of Psychiatry* 154, 775–82.

Lalonde, B.I.D. (1982) 'Quality Assurance', in Austin, M.J. and Hershey, W.E. (eds) *Handbook on Mental Health Administration*, Jossey Bass, San Francisco.

Lamb, H.R (1979) 'The new asylums in the community', *Archives of General Psychiatry* 36, 129–34.

Lamb, H.R. (1980) 'Therapist-case managers more than brokers of services', *Hospital and Community Psychiatry* 31, 762–4.

Lamb, H.R. (1988) 'Deinstitutionalization at the crossroads', *Hospital and Community Psychiatry* 39, 941-5.

Lavender, A. (1985) 'Quality of Care and Staff Practices', in Watts, F.N. (ed.) *New Developments in Clinical Psychology*, John Wiley, London.

Lavender, A. (1987) 'Improving the quality of care on psychiatric hospital rehabilitation wards: a controlled evaluation', *British Journal of Psychiatry* 150, 476-81.

Lavender, A. and Sperlinger, A. (1988) 'Staff Training', in Lavender, A. and Holloway, F. (eds) *Community Care in Practice*, John Wiley, London.

Lavender, A. and Watts, F.N. (1984) 'Assessment in Psychiatric Rehabilitation', in Lindsay, S. and Powell, G.E. (eds) *A Handbook of Clinical Psychology*, Gower, London.

Leach, J. (1979) 'Providing for the Destitute', in Wing, J.K. and Olsen, R. (eds) *Community Care of the Mentally Disabled*, Oxford University Press, Oxford.

Leff, J. (1978) 'Social and Psychological Causes of the Acute Attack', in Wing, J.K. (ed.) *Schizophrenia: Towards a New Synthesis*, Academic Press, London.

Leff, J., Kuipers, L., Berkowitz, R. and Sturgeon, D. (1985) 'A controlled trial of social intervention in the families of schizophrenic patients: Two year follow-up', *British Journal of Psychiatry* 146, 594-600.

Lefley, H.P. (1989) 'Family burden and family stigma in major mental illness', *American Psychologist* 43, 556-60.

Lehman, A.F. (1983) 'The well-being of chronic mental patients', *Archives of General Psychiatry* 40, 369-73.

Liberman, R.P. (ed.) (1988) *Psychiatric Rehabilitation of Chronic Mental Patients*, American Psychiatric Association, Washington.

Liberman, R.P., Mueser, K.T., Wallace, C.J., Jacobs, H.E., Eckman, T. and Mussel, H.K. (1986) 'Training skills in the psychiatrically disabled: learning competence and coping', *Schizophrenia Bulletin* 12, 631-47.

Likert, R. (1961) *New Patterns of Management*, McGraw Hill, New York.

Linn, M.W., Cafey, E.M., Klett, C.J., Hogarty, G.E. and Lamb, H.R. (1979) 'Day treatment and psychotropic drugs in the aftercare of schizophrenic patients', *Archives of General Psychiatry* 36, 1055-66.

Linn, M.W., Klett, C.J. and Caffey, E.M. (1980) 'Foster home characteristics and psychiatric patient outcome', *Archives of General Psychiatry* 39, 129-32.

Linn, M.W., Gurel, L., Williford, W.O., Overall, J., Gurland, B., Laughlin, P. and Barchiesi, A. (1985) 'Nursing home care as an alternative to psychiatric hospitalization', *Archives of General Psychiatry* 39, 129-32.

McAusland, T. (1985) 'Housing for people with long-term psychiatric disabilities - beyond the 24-bedded unit', Occasional Paper, Good Practices in Mental Health, London.

McCarthy, B., (1988) 'The Role of Relatives', in Lavender, A. and Holloway, F. (eds) *Community Care in Practice*, John Wiley, London.

McCarthy, B, Kuipers, L., Hurry, J., Harper, R. and LeSage, A. (1989) 'Counselling the relatives of the adult long-term mentally ill, I. Evaluation of the impact on clients and relatives', *British Journal of Psychiatry* 154, 768–75.

Manchanda, R. and Hirsch, S.R. (1986) 'Low dose maintenance medication for schizophrenia', *British Medical Journal* 293, 515–17.

Mann, S.A. and Cree, W. (1976) 'New long-stay psychiatric patients: a national sample survey of fifteen mental hospitals in England and Wales 1972/3', *Psychological Medicine* 6, 603–16.

Martindale, D. (1987) 'The CARE System', *Working Paper No. 2*, National Unit for Psychiatric Research and Development, London.

Matson, J.L. (1980) 'Behaviour Modification Procedures for Training Chronically Institutionalised Schizophrenics', in Hersen, M., Eisler, R.M., and Millar, P.M. (eds) *Progress in Behaviour Modification*, Academic Press, London.

Menzies, I.E. (1960) 'A case study in the functioning of a social system as a defense against anxiety', *Human Relations* 13, 95–121.

Milne, D. (1985) 'An ecological validation of nurse training in behaviour therapy', *Behavioural Psychotherapy* 13, 14–28.

Milroy, A. (1985) 'Some Reflections on the Experience of the North Derbyshire Mental Health Service Project – Tontine Road, Derbyshire', in McAusland, T, (ed.) *Planning and Monitoring Community Mental Health Centres*, King's Fund Centre, London.

Mitchell, S.F. and Birley, J.L.T. (1983) 'The use of ward support by psychiatric patients in the community', *British Journal of Psychiatry* 142, 9–12.

Morin, R.C. and Seidman, E. (1986) 'A social network approach and the revolving door patient', *Schizophrenia Bulletin* 12, 262–73.

Nagy, M.P., Fisher, G.A. and Tessler, R.C. (1988) 'Effects of facility characteristics on the social adjustment of mentally ill residents of board-and-care homes', *Hospital and Community Psychiatry* 39, 1281–6.

Overtveit, J. (1986) *Organization of Multi-Disciplinary Community Teams*, Brunel Institute of Organization and Social Studies, Uxbridge.

Overtveit, J., Temple, H. and Coleman, R. (1988) 'Organization and Management', in Echlin, R. (ed.) *Community Mental Health Centre Information Pack*, Good Practices in Mental Health, London.

Palazzoli, M.S., Boscolo, L., Cecchin, G. and Prata, G. (1978) *Paradox and Counterparadox*, Jason Aronson, New York.

Parkes, C.M. (1972) *Bereavement*, Penguin, London.

Paul, G.L. and Lentz, R.J. (1977) *Psychosocial Treatment of Chronic Mental Patients: milieu vs. social-learning programs*, Harvard University Press, Harvard, Mass.

Perkins, R.E., King, S.A. and Hollyman, J.A. (1988) 'Resettlement of old long-stay psychiatric patients: the use of the private sector', *British Journal of Psychiatry* 155, 233–8.

Phipps, C. and Liberman, R.P. (1988) 'Community Support', in Liberman, R.P. (ed.) (1988) *Psychiatric Rehabilitation of Chronic Mental Patients*, American Psychiatric Association, Washington.

Pilling, S. (1988a) 'Brian, Living with Schizophrenia in the Community', in West, J. and Spinks, P. (eds) *Case Studies in Clinical Psychology*, Wright, London.

Pilling, S. (1988b) 'Work and the Continuing Care Client', in Lavender, A. and Holloway, F. (eds) *Community Care in Practice*, John Wiley, London.

Platt, S. (1985) 'Measuring the burden of psychiatric illness on the family: an evaluation of some rating scales', *Psychological Medicine* 15, 383-93.

Priest, R.G., Raptopodus, P. and Chou, M.L. (1985) 'The Neglect of the Patient with Chronic Functional Psychosis: the need for further research', in Hegalson, T. (ed.) *The Long-Term Treatment of Functional Psychoses*, Cambridge University Press, Cambridge.

Pritlove, J. (1983) 'Accommodation without resident staff for ex-psychiatric patients', *British Journal of Social Work* 13, 75-92.

Raynes, N.V., Pratt, M.W. and Roses, S. (1979) *'Organizational Structure and the Care of the Mentally Retarded*, Croom Helm, London.

Roberts, J.P. (1980) 'Destructive processes in a therapeutic community', *International Journal of Therapeutic Communities* 1, 159-70.

Robson, M. (1982) *Quality Circles: a practical guide*, Gower, London.

Rogers, E.S., Cohen, B.F., Danley, K.S., Hutchinson, D. and Anthony, W.A. (1986) 'Training mental health workers in psychiatric rehabilitation', *Schizophrenia Bulletin* 12, 709-18.

Rosie, J.S. (1987) 'Partial hospitalisation: a review of recent literature', *Hospital and Community Psychiatry* 38, 1291-9.

Ryan, P. (1979) 'Residential Care for the Mentally Disabled', in Wing, J.K. and Olsen, R. (eds) *Community Care for the Mentally Disabled*, Oxford University Press, Oxford.

Sayce, L. (1987) *Community Mental Health Centres: Report of the Annual Conference*, National Unit for Psychiatric Research and Development, London.

Sechrest, L. and Rosenblatt, A. (1988) 'Evaluating Peer Review', in Stricker, G. and Rodriguez, A.R. (eds) (1988) *Handbook of Quality Assurance in Mental Health*, Plenum, New York.

Segal S.P. and Moyles, E.W. (1979) 'Management style and institutional dependency in sheltered care', *Social Psychiatry* 14, 159-65.

Shaw, C. (1986) *Introducing Quality Assurance*, King's Fund Centre, London.

Shepherd, G. (1978) 'Social skills training: the generalization problem – some further data', *Behaviour Research and Therapy* 16, 287-8.

Shepherd, G. (1984) *Institutional Care and Rehabilitation*, Longman, London.

Shepherd, G. (1988a) 'Practical aspects of the management of negative symptoms', *International Journal of Mental Health* 16, 75-97.

Shepherd, G. (1988b) 'Evaluation and Service Planning', in Lavender, A.

and Holloway, F. (eds) *Community Care in Practice*, John Wiley, London.

Shepherd, G. (1989a) 'The value of work in the 1980s', *Psychiatric Bulletin* 13, 231-3.

Shepherd, G. (1989b) 'Care of the chronic mentally ill', *Current Opinion in Psychiatry* 2, 291-5.

Sherman, P. (1988) 'A micro-based decision support system for managing aggressive case management programs for treatment-resistant clients', in Greenhalgh, J. (ed.) *State Management Information Systems in the West: Trends and Developments*, Western Interstate Commission for Higher Education, Boulder, Co.

Silverstone, T. and Turner, P. (1988) *Drug Treatments in Psychiatry*, Routledge & Kegan Paul, London.

Simpson, C.J., Hyde, C.E. and Faragher, E.B. (1989) 'The chronically mentally ill in community facilities: a study of quality of life', *British Journal of Psychiatry* 154, 77-82.

Smith, J.V. and Birchwood, M.J. (1987) 'Specific and non-specific effects of educational interventions with families living with a schizophrenic patient', *British Journal of Psychiatry* 150, 645-52.

Social Services Committee (1985) *Second Report (session 1984-5) on community care with special respect to adult mentally ill and handicapped people*, HMSO, London.

South East Thames Health Authority (1988) *First Things First*, Outset Publishing, East Sussex.

Stanton, A. and Schwartz, M. (1954) *The Mental Hospital*, Basic Books, New York.

Stein, L.I. and Test, M.A. (1980) 'Alternatives to mental hospital treatment', *Archives of General Psychiatry* 37, 392-412.

Strachan, A. (1986) 'Family intervention for the rehabilitation of schizophrenia. Toward protection and coping', *Schizophrenia Bulletin* 12, 678-98.

Strauss, J.S. (1986) 'What does rehabilitation accomplish?', *Schizophrenia Bulletin* 12, 720-3.

Stricker, G. and Rodriguez, A.R. (eds) (1988) *Handbook of Quality Assurance in Mental Health*, Plenum, New York.

Sturt, E., Wykes, T. and Creer, C. (1982) 'Demographic, social and clinical characteristics of the sample', in Wing, J.K. (ed.) *Long-term Community Care: experience in a London borough*, Psychological Medicine Monograph Supplement 2.

Talbot, J.A. and Glick, I.D. (1986) 'The in-patient care of the chronically mentally ill', *Schizophrenia Bulletin* 12, 129-40.

Tarrier, N. (1988) 'Family involvement', *Current Opinion in Psychiatry* 1, 210-15.

Thornicroft, G. (1989) Correspondence, *British Medical Journal* 299, 1525.

Timms, P.W. and Fry, A.H. (1989) 'Homelessness and mental illness', *Health Trends* 21, 70-1.

Towell, D. and McAusland, T. (1984) Psychiatric services in transition',

*Health and Social Services Journal* (25 October) Centre 8 Supplement.

Tressler, R.C. and Goldman, H.H. (1982) *The Chronically Mentally Ill. Assessing Community Support Programs*, Ballinger, Cambridge, Mass.

Vaughan, C.E. and Leff, J.P. (1976) 'The influence of family and social factors on the course of psychiatric illness', *British Journal of Psychiatry* 129, 125–38.

Vaughan, P.J. (1985) 'Developments in psychiatric day care', *British Journal of Psychiatry* 147, 1–4.

Wallace, C.J. (1986) 'Functional assessment in rehabilitation', *Schizophrenia Bulletin* 12, 604–24.

Walsh, D. (1985) 'Case Registers for Monitoring Treatment Outcome in Chronic Functional Psychoses', in Hegalson, T. (ed.) *The Long-Term Treatment of Functional Psychoses*, Cambridge University Press, Cambridge.

Watts, F.N. and Bennett, D.H. (eds) (1983a) *Theory and Practice of Psychiatric Rehabilitation*, John Wiley, London.

Watts, F.N. and Bennett, D.H. (1983b) 'Management of the Staff Team', in Watts, F.N. and Bennett, D.H. (eds) *Theory and Practice of Psychiatric Rehabilitation*, John Wiley, London.

Whitehead, C.S. (1987) *Co-ordinated Aftercare for Schizophrenia. Report of a Pilot Study*, Salford Health Authority, Salford.

Wing, J.K. and Brown, G.W. (1970) *Institutionalism and Schizophrenia*, Cambridge University Press, Cambridge.

Wing, J.K. and Furlong, R. (1986) 'A haven for the severely disabled within the context of a comprehensive psychiatric service', *British Journal of Psychiatry* 149, 449–57.

Wing, J.K. and Morris, B. (1981) 'Clinical Basis of Rehabilitation', in Wing, J.K. and Morris, B. (eds) *Handbook of Psychiatric Rehabilitation*, Oxford University Press, Oxford.

Wittlin, B.J. (1988) 'Practical Psychopharmocology', in Liberman, R.P. (ed.) *Psychiatric Rehabilitation of Chronic Mental Patients*, American Psychiatric Association, Washington.

Wolfensberger, W. (1980) 'The Definition of Normalization: Update, problems, disagreements and misunderstandings', in Flynn, R.J. and Nitsch, K.E. (eds) *Normalization, Social Integration and Community Services*, University Park Press, Baltimore.

Wolfensberger, W. (1983) 'Social role valorization: a proposed new term for the principle of normalization', *Mental Retardation* 21, 234–9.

Wolfensberger, W. and Glenn, L. (1973) *Program Analysis of Service Systems (PASS) Handbook*, National Institute on Mental Retardation, Toronto.

Woods, P.A., Higson, P.J. and Tannahill, M.M. (1984) 'Token economy programmes with chronic patients. The importance of direct measurement and objective evaluation of long-term maintenance', *Behaviour Research and Therapy* 22, 41–51.

Wooff, K. and Goldberg, D.P. (1988) 'Further observations on the practice of community care in Salford: differences between community psychiatric nurses and mental health social workers', *British Journal of Psychiatry* 153, 30–7.

Wykes, T. (1982) 'A hostel-ward for new long-stay patients: an evaluative study of a "ward in a house" ', in Wing, J.K. (ed.) 'Long-term Community Care: experience in a London borough', *Psychological Medicine Monograph Supplement 2.*

Wykes, T., Creer, C. and Sturt, E. (1982) 'Needs and the Deployment of Services', in Wing, J.K. (ed.) 'Long-term Community Care: experience in a London borough', *Psychological Medicine Monograph Supplement 2.*

Zipple, A.M., Carling, P. and McDonald, J. (1987) 'A rehabilitation response to the call for asylum', *Schizophrenia Bulletin* 13, 539–45.

Zusman, J. (1988) 'Quality assurance in mental health care', *Hospital and Community Psychiatry* 39, 1286–90.

# NAME INDEX

# SUBJECT INDEX